KU-264-211

Pembrokeshire Coast Path

Wales Coast Path: St Dogmaels to Amroth

Brian John

Aurum

in association with

Cyngor Cefn Gwlad Cymru
Countryside Council for Wales

Acknowledgements

Walking the full length of the Pembrokeshire Coast Path for the first edition of this book brought me very great pleasure, as have my subsequent expeditions connected with the revision process. I hope that those who use the book will sense my enjoyment and will share my instinct for field investigation and desktop enquiry. I thank my wife Inger, who has been with me on many of my outings and who has dropped me off and picked me up on more occasions than I care to remember. I have received great help from the staff of the National Park Authority, and particular thanks go to Dave Maclachlan, the National Trail Officer, who has kindly drawn my attention to changes large and small, and whose knowledge of the Path is second to none. Finally, I thank Graham Coster, publisher of the National Trail Guides, for his encouragement and patience, and Brenda Updegraff for her ability to turn scruffy notes into tidy text.

This fully revised and updated edition first published 2012 by Aurum Press Ltd
7 Greenland Street, London NW1 0ND • www.aurumpress.co.uk
in association with Natural England and Cyngor Cefn Gwlad Cymru, the Countryside Council of Wales
www.naturalengland.org.uk • www.ccgc.gov.uk • www.nationaltrail.co.uk
First published in 1990

Text copyright © 1990, 1997, 2001, 2004, 2008, 2010, 2012 by Aurum Press Ltd
and Natural England
Photographs copyright © 2012 the photographer or agency as follows: 2–3, 11, 12–13, 20, 22–23, 38–39, 48, 60, 79, 80, 92, 124 and 139 PCNPA; 22–23, 125 PCNPA; 16 Pete Newman; 21 Rory Francis; 52 Brian John; 111 Corbis; 115 Countryside Council for Wales; 127 Pembrokeshire Coastal Photography; 132 Lucrezya; 1, 15, 27, 30, 36, 43, 44–45, 55, 56, 63, 64, 68–69, 71, 72, 74–75, 86, 88, 97, 99, 100, 109, 140–41 and 144 Alamy. All other photographs Martin Trelawny copyright © Natural England.

OS Ordnance Survey® This product includes mapping data licensed from Ordnance Survey® with the permission of the Controller of Her Majesty's Stationery Office. © Crown copyright 2010. All rights reserved. Licence number 43453U. Ordnance Survey is a registered trade mark and the Ordnance Survey Symbol, Explorer and Outdoor Leisure are trade marks of Ordnance Survey, the National Mapping Agency of Great Britain.

ISBN 978 1 84513 782 3

Book design by Robert Updegraff • Printed in China

Cover photograph: *Stackpole Quay*
Half-title page: *Boats at Solva*
Title page: *Rock formations at Marloes*

Aurum Press want to ensure that these National Trail Guides are always as up to date as possible – but stiles collapse, pubs close and bus services change all the time. If, on walking this path, you discover any important changes that future walkers need to be aware of, do let us know. Either go to our website, **www.aurumpress.co.uk/trailguides**, and add your comments, or, if you take the trouble to drop us a line to:

Trail Guides, Aurum Press, 7 Greenland Street, London NW1 0ND,

we'll send you a free guide of your choice as thanks.

Contents

How to use this guide

This guide to the 186-mile (299-kilometre) Pembrokeshire Coast Path is in three parts:

• The introduction, with an historical background to the area and advice for walkers.

• The Coast Path itself, split into twelve chapters, with maps opposite the description for each route section. The distances noted at the start of each chapter represent the total walking length of the Pembrokeshire Coast Path, including sections through towns and villages. There may be some variation, depending on whether firing ranges are open. An estimate of the total ascent for that section is given, along with the altitude of the highest point you will encounter that day. This part of the guide also includes information on places of interest as well as a number of short walks which can be taken around each part of the path. Key sites are numbered both in the text and on the maps to make it easier to follow the route description.

• The last part indicates useful information, such as local transport, accommodation and organisations involved with the Pembrokeshire Coast Path.

The maps have been prepared by the Ordnance Survey® for this trail guide using 1:25 000 Explorer™ maps as a base. The line of the Pembrokeshire Coast Path is shown in yellow, with the status of each section of the trail – footpath or bridleway, for example – shown in green underneath (see key on inside front cover). These rights-of-way markings also indicate the precise alignment of the Pembrokeshire Coast Path, which walkers should follow. In some cases, the yellow line on these maps may show a route that is different from that shown on older maps; walkers are recommended to follow the yellow route in this guide, which will be the route that is waymarked with the distinctive acorn symbol ♟ used for all National Trails. Any parts of the Pembrokeshire Coast Path that may be difficult to follow on the ground are clearly highlighted in the route description, and important points to watch for are marked with letters in each chapter, both in the text and on the maps. *Some maps start on a right-hand page and continue on the left-hand page – black arrows (➤) at the edge of the maps indicate the start point.*

Should there be a need to divert the Pembrokeshire Coast Path from the route shown in this guide, for maintenance work or because the route has had to be changed, walkers are advised to follow any waymarks or signs along the path.

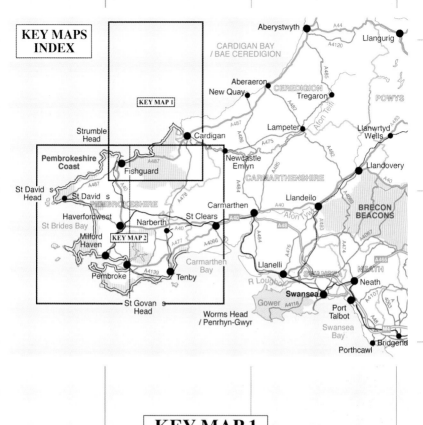

KEY MAPS INDEX

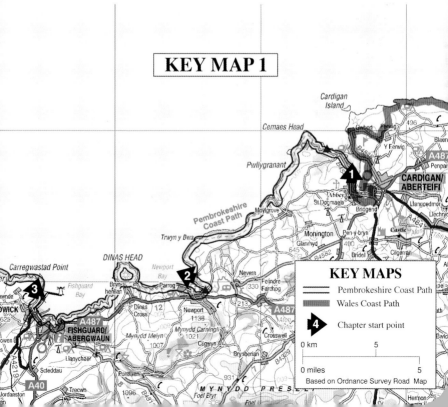

KEY MAP 1

KEY MAPS

——— Pembrokeshire Coast Path

▓▓▓ Wales Coast Path

4 ▸ Chapter start point

0 km   5

0 miles   5

Based on Ordnance Survey Road Map

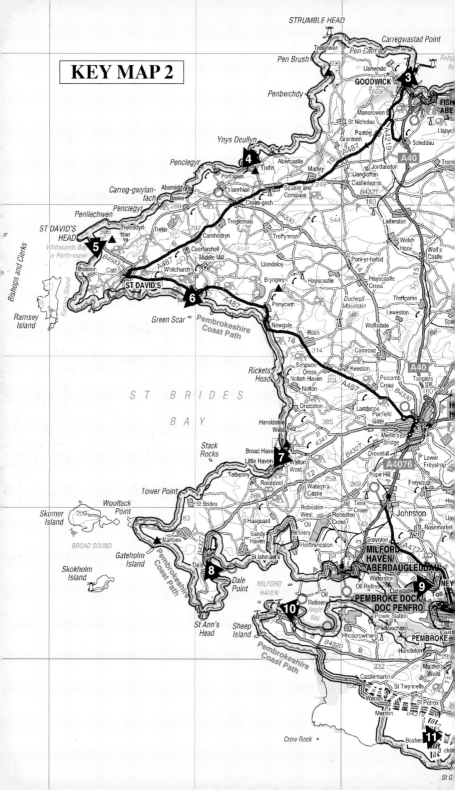

Distance checklist

This list will assist you in calculating the distances between your proposed overnight accommodation and in checking your progress along the walk.

location	miles	km	
	approx. distance from previous location		
	miles	km	
St Dogmaels	0	0	
Poppit Sands	1.3	2.7	
Ceibwr Bay (for Moylgrove 0.8 miles/1.3 km)	5.6	9.0	
Newport (Parrog)	8.6	13.8	
Cwm-yr-Eglwys	3.1	5.0	
Fishguard (via Dinas Head)	7.0	11.3	
Goodwick (Harbour Heights)	2.3	3.7	
Aber Bach (for St Nicholas 1.4 miles/2.3 km)	11.3	18.2	
Abercastle	3.3	5.3	
Trefin	2.7	4.3	
Porth-gain	1.7	2.7	
Whitesands Bay	9.5	15.3	
Porth Clais (for St David's 1.1 miles/1.8 km)	6.3	10.1	
Solva	5.8	9.3	
Newgale	4.3	6.9	
Nolton Haven (for Nolton 0.6 miles/1.0 km)	3.0	4.8	
Broad Haven	3.5	5.6	
Little Haven	0.8	1.3	
St Bride's Haven	5.4	8.7	
Musselwick (for Marloes 0.7 miles/1.1 km)	2.3	3.7	
Marloes Sands (for Marloes 1.3 miles/2.1 km)	4.0	6.4	
Dale (via St Ann's Head)	7.8	12.6	
Monk Haven (for St Ishmael's 0.7 miles/1.1 km)	2.5	4.0	via Pickleridge
	4.7*	7.6	via Mullock Bridge
(Sandy Haven) East side of Sandyhaven Pill (for Herbrandston 0.9 miles/1.4 km)	3.4	5.5	via stepping stones
	7.2*	11.6	via Rickeston Bridge and Herbrandston
Hakin	3.9	6.3	
Milford Haven	0.7	1.1	
Neyland	5.3	8.5	

Thorn Island Fort, near the mouth of Milford Haven. This fort was built around 1850 as one of the key structures defending the waterway and the Royal Naval Dockyard.

location	approx. distance from previous location		
	miles	km	
Pembroke Dock	2.9	4.7	
Pembroke	2.8	4.5	
Angle	11.3	18.2	
Castlemartin	10.3	16.6	
Bosherston	5.0*	8.0	via Sampson Cross
	7.5	12.1	via Stack Rocks and St Govan's Chapel
Freshwater East (0.6 miles/1.0 km to village)	6.9*	11.1	via lily pools to Broad Haven
	9.1	14.6	via St Govan's Head to Broad Haven
(Castlemartin to Freshwater East via St Govan's Head, avoiding Bosherston 10.5* miles/16.6 km)			
Manorbier Bay (for Manorbier 0.4 miles/0.6 km)	3.5	5.6	
Lydstep Haven (for Lydstep 0.4 miles/0.6 km)	3.0	4.8	
Penally	2.4	3.9	via A4139
	3.4*	5.5	via Giltar Point
Tenby	2.1	3.4	
Saundersfoot	4.1	6.6	
Wiseman's Bridge	1.3	2.1	
Amroth	1.9	3.1	

* = not used for overall distance

Broad Haven

PART ONE
Introduction

Introducing the Pembrokeshire coast

The Pembrokeshire Coast Path was designated as a National Trail in order to allow free public access to one of Europe's most magnificent and varied coastlines. Where possible, the route runs close to the cliff edge, but this is by no means a simple cliffed coast and there are stretches that run along, or close to, sandy beaches; stretches far enough inland to be out of sight and sound of the sea; and stretches on the shores of the deep natural harbour of Milford Haven. On every section of the footpath you will encounter creeks, coves, coastal valleys and sandy beaches, and you are seldom far from civilisation. Indeed, the string of little coastal villages discovered at regular intervals by the Coast Path walker gives this coastline much of its charm, adding a sense of scale, intimacy and warmth to cliff scenery that might otherwise be somewhat intimidating.

The landscape of Pembrokeshire is immensely ancient. All the rocks underlying the land surface are more than 300 million years old, and in the cliffs you can see, in varying colours, textures and patterns, the story of Britain's evolution over some 700 million years of geological time. The relations between rocks and cliff scenery are described in more detail on page 32. Here and there the events of the Ice Age have dramatically affected the coastline, with the creation of deep valleys and the dumping of glacial and other sediments.

For the most part the inland landscape, truncated by the coastal cliffs, is flat or gently undulating, and these ancient platform surfaces have themselves been partly fashioned by the work of the sea at times of higher sea levels millions of years ago. In places the youngest platforms, around 100 feet (30 metres) above the present sea level, are quite spectacular – as around Flimston, on the southern limestone coast, or in the Marloes–Dale area. Elsewhere, the old platforms have been modified by river action and given a gently undulating appearance. And in other areas, especially in the north, the uplands of Pembrokeshire extend right out to the coast, giving rise to cliffs over 330 feet (100 metres) high.

The wildlife of Pembrokeshire is superb, and indeed it is because of the wonderful displays of spring wild flowers and the abundance of seabirds that this coastal environment is so greatly valued. The Pembrokeshire air is clean, the light is clear, and the water has a blueness that never ceases to amaze visitors from the North Sea coasts. All of the coastal cliff tops are transformed in the months of April, May and June by sheets of wild flowers, and at the same time seabirds are nesting in their thousands – for the most part on the offshore islands but also to an increasing extent on mainland cliffs. Later in the year the wildlife is less abundant and the colours less exotic, but walking the path during the high summer months is an experience to be treasured none the less.

In this guide I have tried to emphasise the great variety of natural features and wildlife to be seen along the coast, but we must not forget the human influence, which is everywhere apparent. This is – and has been for many centuries – a farmed landscape. The twin activities of farming and fishing have provided the staples of the local diet until very recently. The coastal settlements were the focal points of Pembrokeshire life, for the sea was above all a provider of food. But it was also the major highway before the arrival of good road and rail communications about a century ago. There are many reminders of this maritime tradition – the cromlechs of the Neolithic folk who arrived by sea, the promontory forts of the Iron Age immigrants, the churches and chapels of the seafaring Celtic saints and their followers, the coastal castles of the Norman invaders, and the Victorian defences built to repel a French invasion force that never arrived. The little quays, lime kilns, breakwaters and warehouses that feature prominently in the coastal settlements remind us also of the long tradition of shipbuilding and coastal trading which has now been overtaken by the new tradition of seafaring for fun.

One cultural feature that will be immediately apparent to the observant map-reading coastal walker is the predominance of Welsh place names in the north, contrasting with the predominance of English place names in the south. And scattered along the whole of the Pembrokeshire coast are Scandinavian names adding spice to the mixture – for example, Ramsey, Skomer, Grassholm, Musselwick, Hubberston and Gosker. The Welsh–English split is a matter of early medieval history, owing its origins to the successful colonisation of South Pembrokeshire by the Normans and their followers, and the successful resistance of the Welsh inhabitants of the north. For more than 900 years the two communities have lived side by side more or less amicably. The divide, or *Landsker*, which separated them in the Middle Ages, is still in more or less its original position, and still traceable.

The Industrial Revolution came late to Pembrokeshire and had an impact only in small coastal pockets. Places such as Porth-gain, Abereiddi, Pembroke Dock and Wiseman's Bridge still bear its scars, but the impact of the coal era has been

One of the spectacular sea caves at the southern end of Ramsey Island.

Rocky outcrops projecting through the sandy beach at Freshwater West, on the west-facing coast of the Castlemartin peninsula.

lessened over time as the little mines and spoil heaps of the Pembrokeshire coalfield have been reduced to fragmentary ruins and grassy mounds. The latest episodes in Pembrokeshire's history still make dramatic impacts on the landscape. For example, the Milford Haven oil industry has developed over the last 50 years on a scale out of all proportion to anything that has gone before. But nothing is for ever. Already four of the original oil installations have closed, and the first Pembroke power station has been demolished. A new generation of Liquefied Natural Gas installations is now being developed and two of the original oil jetties have been refurbished. The holiday industry, too, waxes and wanes as tastes and economic circumstances change. Caravan parks, self-catering chalets, marinas and leisure parks are now essential features of the Pembrokeshire scene. Who knows how long they will last? The coastal communities have seen it all before. Over centuries of change they have adapted and survived on this fascinating interface between land and sea that we know as the Pembrokeshire coast.

Hardly any puffins nest on the mainland, but there are sizeable colonies on the islands of Skomer and Skokholm.

History of the Coast Path

The Pembrokeshire Coast Path was officially opened on 16 May 1970 by Wynford Vaughan Thomas, then President of the Council for the Protection of Rural Wales. Following the designation of the Pembrokeshire Coast National Park in 1952, the author and naturalist Ronald Lockley surveyed a route for a long-distance footpath following the coast, and his report for the Countryside Commission (now replaced by the Countryside Council for Wales) was enthusiastically accepted and acted upon in the summer of 1953. There were immense complications in designating the path; some sections were on existing rights-of-way, but the great majority of the coastline was, of course, in private hands, and hundreds of new rights-of-way had to be negotiated

with individual landowners. The great majority of them were cooperative, and agreed to public access as long as new fences, walls and stiles could be built to prevent any undue disturbance to local farming activities. In many cases farmers actually benefited from the improvement of clifftop fencing, and from the addition of steps and bridges in awkward locations. Some landowners proved difficult to deal with, and to this day there are a few places where the footpath heads unexpectedly away from the coast or sends the walker off on a convoluted detour. In many places the path had to be hacked out of the 'jungle' or created with the help of a miniature bulldozer. More than 100 footbridges were built, 479 numbered stiles installed, thousands of steps cut into steep and slippery slopes, dangerous cliff sections avoided and marked, and fingerposts erected; and landowners and members of the public were reassured that all of this 'damage' was in a good cause. It is hardly surprising that these tasks took 17 years to complete.

Inevitably, the path still has its problem areas. Now, since the completion of the Cleddau Bridge across Milford Haven, it is possible to walk from St Dogmaels to Amroth without a break. But the Coast Path was not designated through the built-up areas of Milford Haven, Neyland, Pembroke Dock, Pembroke, Tenby and Saundersfoot, and there are still long and frustrating detours around the Castlemartin Range, Manorbier Range, Penally Camp and the Pembroke Power Station site. In some places the path was never actually constructed along its designated route; elsewhere stretches of the marked route have proved unacceptable to walkers and they have made new routes of their own.

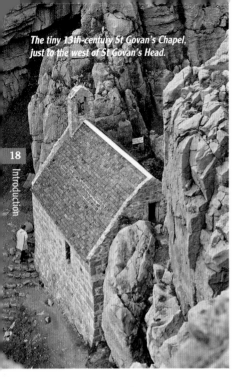

The tiny 13th-century St Govan's Chapel, just to the west of St Govan's Head.

to walk the whole of the coast of Wales, for a distance about 850 miles (1367 km). However, the Pembrokeshire Coast Path was the inspiration for the Wales Coast Path project, not simply because of its beauty but also because of its extraordinary geological and ecological diversity. It is also a designated part of the International Appalachian Trail which celebrates the transatlantic geological links between western Britain and the eastern seaboard of North America."

Planning your walk and accommodation

Walking the Pembrokeshire Coast Path *can* be completed in under a week if you are in a great hurry, but such speed is not recommended! Better to take 12 days if you are fit and more if you are not. Remember that if you walk the whole route you will climb 30,347 feet (9,250 metres) in the process. If you really want to enjoy the path, return to it again and again, savouring your favourite sections in different weathers and at different seasons.

I would not recommend any of the full sections of this path to disabled people, horseriders or cyclists. Steep slopes, dangerous proximity to the cliff edge, and occasional stiles, kissing-gates and flights of steps mean that this is mostly a path for those who are reasonably fit, properly equipped and well shod. However, there are innumerable access points in addition to those identified as the start/stop points at the beginning and end of each chapter of this book. Details of cycleways, wheelchair routes

The Coast Path is now 40 years old, and it is inevitable that some rationalisation should have occurred. Its designated length is 167 miles (269 km), but since 1970 a number of Footpath Diversion Orders have lengthened it. For all practical purposes its length is now 186 miles (299 km). Stiles are being removed (only 55 are left) and at the last count there were 453 gates to pass through. In the towns the best routes for walkers are shown by urban waymarks. Look for the acorns! If you enjoy and explore the Pembrokeshire coast properly, and visit the peninsulas of Lydstep Head, Dinas Island, St Govan's Head, and the Deer Park at Martin's Haven, you will actually walk in excess of 200 miles (320 km). Try not to miss out on any of it; the beautiful Pembrokeshire coast is quite incomparable.

With the official opening of the Wales Coast Path in 2012, it is now possible and gentler sections can be obtained from the National Park Authority. The only significant bridleway length is the permissive inland route between Stack Rocks and St Govans. Car parks, youth hostels, inns and other facilities are marked on the maps that follow.

If you are walking a long stretch of the route which entails overnight stops, try to book accommodation or camping space beforehand, especially in the peak holiday months. Accommodation lists and other helpful leaflets can be obtained from tourist information centres, from the county council tourism unit, and of course via web searches.

Planning your walk is now much easier than it was, thanks to the five 'walkers' bus services' operating a timetable to many access points on the National Trail. Further details are given on page 144.

Safety precautions

Conditions are not dangerous if you walk carefully and take proper account of weather conditions and the state of the ground underfoot; but remember that fatal accidents do occur on the cliffs of Pembrokeshire, usually because walkers take unnecessary risks and fail to appreciate that cliff tops and cliff faces are extremely dangerous. You are more likely to have an accident if you have a heavy pack and are tired at the end of a long day. Make sure that somebody knows your walking plans and your estimated arrival time, especially outside the main holiday season; some stretches of the path are very isolated and access is difficult. Pay particular attention to those parts where cliff-falls and landslips are common; you may find that short sections of the path have been eroded away, leaving unmarked sheer drops

The lifeboat station at St Justinian's.
Ramsey Island can be seen on the skyline.

The Coast Path between Morfa Head and Newport. The summit of Carningli can be seen in the distance.

variable. It is always a good idea to carry a sweater, an anorak and a set of waterproofs. Wear good strong walking boots if you can afford them. And if you are walking alone, *always* carry a whistle and a bivouac sheet or some other protection in case you suffer a serious accident when you are in a remote spot. The first section of the path (St Dogmaels to Newport) is very tough, with no liquid refreshments en route; make sure that you carry plenty to drink.

A word about distances and tides. In some bays you can walk on the beach instead of the Coast Path if the tide is out; but carry a set of tide tables and do not allow yourself to be cut off by a rising tide. At the Gann (near Dale) and at Sandy Haven, delicate timing is needed in order to cross river mouths when the tide is low; if you get it wrong long detours are the inevitable penalty. In several other bays and estuaries short sections of the Trail may be flooded by extreme spring tides.

Finally, good timing is also required if you want to walk the 'Range East' part of the Castlemartin Range. In general, the stretch from Stack Rocks to Broad Haven is open at weekends during the summer months, but on weekdays you may find it closed until 5 pm and have to use the inland Castlemartin Range Trail, with short sections of road and long field sections. There may be cattle in the fields. If you are lucky (or well organised) you may be able to join a guided walk with National Park staff along the cliff tops of Range West. Full information about firing schedules and access can be obtained either from the Range Office (01646 662367) or from National Park

that can be lethal if you are walking in bad light or heavy rain. If no detour has been established, then the national park rangers are probably unaware of the cliff-fall. Please make a note of the grid reference and inform the National Park Authority. Here and there you encounter badger holes, or pits or crevasses in the footpath which may be signs of subsidence on the cliff edge. Beware of extreme wind turbulence, especially when there is an onshore wind blowing. Please ensure that dogs and children are kept under proper control. Never allow small children to run ahead of you or play games on clifftop sections of the Coast Path.

The weather encountered on the Pembrokeshire coast is nothing if not information centres. Please note that there is *no* right of unaccompanied access to Range West at any time.

Do not be put off by any of the above. The path is not dangerous if you observe a few simple rules and, if you are well prepared and careful, you will enjoy the Pembrokeshire coast at its best.

Access for disabled visitors

In recent years the National Park Authority, in conjunction with other bodies, has made strenuous efforts to improve access for those with mobility problems and other disabilities. For example, there are now several long sections of the trail which are entirely free of stiles, for example between

Pwllderi and Pwllcaerog and between Skrinkle and Amroth. Some of these are called 'Adventure Chair Paths'. Significant lengths of the path (designated as 'Wheelchair Paths') are also surfaced to a standard suitable for wheelchairs, for example between Iron Bridge (Afon Nyfer) and the old lifeboat station at Cwm (Newport); the Marine Walk between Lower Town Fishguard and Goodwick; and Saundersfoot to Wiseman's Bridge. Finally, there are many sections of the trail which are identified as 'Gentle Walks' and 'Not so Gentle Walks' suitable for various levels of fitness; these are listed in National Trail publications. Comprehensive information and guidance is now available from National Park information centres and for download via the web.

Mixed deciduous woodlands such as this at Coedlan yn ymyl Pontfaen, Cwm Gwaun, are found in many of the sheltered valleys around the Pembrokeshire coast

The sheltered cove of Cwm-yr-Eglwys, with the graveyard and the church of St Brynach, which was almost destroyed in the great storm of 1859.

PART TWO
Pembrokeshire Coast Path

St Dogmaels to Newport (Parrog)

15½ miles (25 km)

passing Poppit Sands and Ceibwr Bay

Ascent 4,068 feet (1,240 metres)
Highest point 574 feet (175 metres)

The Ceredigion Coast Path and the Pembrokeshire Coast Path are both parts of the long-distance Wales Coast Path. If you are coming into Pembrokeshire from the Ceredigion coast, pick up the WCP signs and waymarks (dragonshells) from Cardigan Bridge. Cross the bridge and turn right towards St Dogmael's, looking for the signs on to the bridleway that leads inland after 65 yards (60 metres). The route leaves the bridleway after 330 yards (300 metres) and the waymarks lead the walker around fields and into the back of St Dogmael's. Walk through the village, pass the ruined abbey and then cross the main road to follow the elevated estuary path with views along the river. This will bring you to the official start of the Pembrokeshire Coast Path.

This stretch of the Pembrokeshire Coast Path is a taxing one, but walkers are amply rewarded for their efforts by continuous contact with wild and beautiful cliff scenery. Some of the highest cliffs in Pembrokeshire are encountered on this stretch, and walkers will climb 4,068 feet (1,240 metres) before they reach Newport. If you are not fit, allow a good long day for this walk and assume that it will take you more than eight hours. Carry plenty to drink. As elsewhere on the Coast Path, the route is well marked and well trodden, and you are unlikely to go astray.

Cardigan **1** is well served by buses from all the neighbouring towns. To start on the trail proper, you need to get to the village of St Dogmaels, served by regular bus services from Cardigan and by the Poppit Rocket bus.

The marked start of the Pembrokeshire Coast Path **A** is next to the landing stage at the northern end of St Dogmaels, an ancient fishing village whose houses cling to the steep hillsides above the Teifi Valley. The first 3 miles (4.5 km) follow roads and country lanes, but for 440 yards (400 metres) or so there is a new off-road route. Once past Webley Hotel there are fine views of the shifting sands and mud banks of the estuary; to the

A view of the high cliff coast at Ceibwr Bay, with Pen yr Afr visible in the distance.

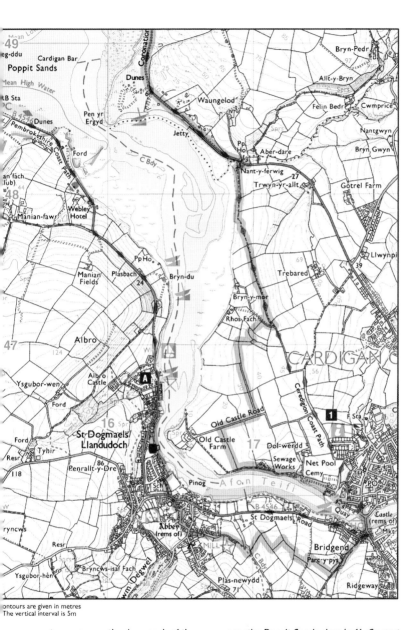

ontours are given in metres
The vertical interval is 5m

west you can see the deep gash of the Cippyn channel cut across the headland by glacial meltwater about 200,000 years ago. The original first sign for the 'Pembrokeshire Coast Long Distance Footpath' is on the wall at the roadside

near the Poppit Sands shop/café. Go past the beach track and keep to the road. As the road climbs to over 425 feet (130 metres), you will have fine views across the estuary, towards Cardigan Island and around the full sweep of Cardigan Bay.

At Allt-y-goed Farm **B** you leave the country lane and start on the footpath by passing through a gate near the cattle grid.

Cemaes Head **2** is a nature reserve and SSSI managed by Wildlife Trust South and West Wales. The headland itself is low and unspectacular – the cliffs are much more impressive to the south of Craig yr Odyn, but as you round the head a wonderful vista opens up towards the south-west, with views of Dinas Island, Pen Caer and

Strumble Head (look for the flashing light). The cliffs in this area are almost vertical and over 440 feet (135 metres) high. Continuing south along the path, you will pass the point at which the footpath leading back to Cnwcau or Cippyn leaves the Coast Path **C**.

As you continue south-westwards you pass the highest point on the whole of the National Trail – over 575 feet (175 metres). The cliffs are quite magnificent, revealing textbook examples of ancient

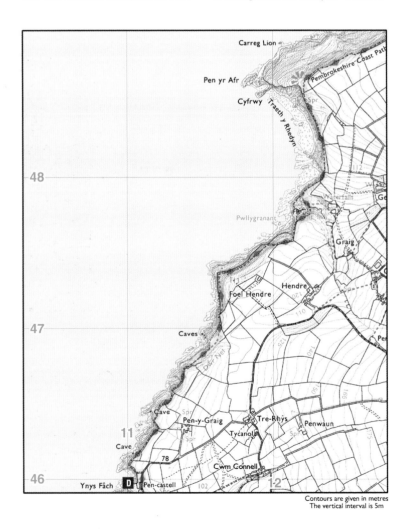

Contours are given in metres
The vertical interval is 5m

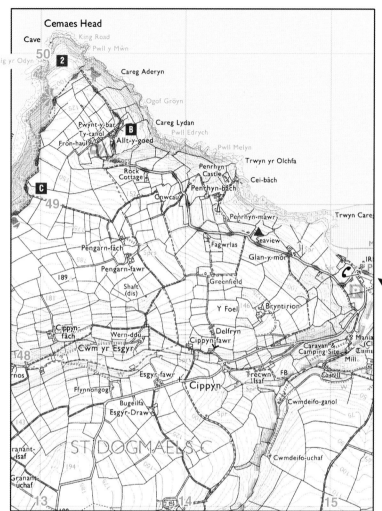

Cemaes Head

Cave

Craig yr Odyn

King Road
Pwll y Mwn

50

2

Careg Aderyn

Ogof Gröyn

Pwynt-y-bar
Ty-canol
Fron-haul

Careg Lydan
Pwll Edrych

B

Allt-y-goed

Pwll Melyn

Trwyn yr Olchfa

Rock
Cottage

Penrhyn
Castle

Cei-bâch

C

49

Cnwcau

Penrhyn-bâch

Penrhyn-mawr

Trwyn Care

Pengarn-fâch

Fagwrlas

Seaview

Glan-y-môr

27

St Dogmaels to Newport

Pengarn-fawr

189

Shaft
(dis)

Greenfield

Y Foel

Bryntirion

IR
P

C

Cippyn-
fâch

Wern-ddu

Delfryn

Cippyn-fawr

Cwm yr Esgyr

Caravan &
Camping Site

Mania
(C)
Tum
Mill

nos

Esgyr-fawr

Trecwn
Isaf

FB

Castell

Ffynnongog

Cippyn

Spr

Bugeilfa
Esgyr-Draw

Cwmdeifo-ganol

ranant-
isaf

ST DOGMAELS C

194

Granant-
uchaf

Cwmdeifo-uchaf

13

14

15

Contours are given in metres
The vertical interval is 5m

folding and faulting structures in the rocks. You pass the pretty cove of Pwllygranant and eventually approach Ceibwr Bay. You pass inland of Pen-castell **D**, cross the lane and follow the edge of the field. Beware of boggy conditions as you descend into the valley. Ceibwr's stone footbridge replaces a much smaller concrete one washed away by a flood in 1993.

The delightful modern footbridge at Ceibwr, built with stone slabs on supporting stone pillars.

Ceibwr **3** was once the port serving Moylgrove and the surrounding farming community. Note the ruined lime kiln near the mouth of the stream. The bay is now in the care of the National Trust. Fulmars nest on the cliffs here, and on several other cliff sections between Ceibwr and Newport. This bird is extending its range all the time along the Pembrokeshire coast; a century ago there was only one colony in the whole of Britain. There is also a breeding colony of house martins on the cliffs south of Ceibwr **3**.

Pwll y Wrach (the Witches Cauldron) **4** is one of the finest features of marine

erosion on the Pembrokeshire coast. The cauldron itself is a collapsed cave, formed where the sea has been able to pick out soft crumbling shales and sandstones along a fault. There are steep gradients on both sides of the valley. Classic cliff scenery appears again in the great amphitheatre of cliffs looking down on the eastern end of Traeth Cell-Howel, where there are fine examples of rotational slumps with many thousands of tons of rock slipping downwards in a series of gigantic steps. The cliff here **E** is being eroded, so take

Look out for ...

... the mermaid statue at St Dogmael's **A** commemorating a famous folk-tale; the great cliffs between Cemaes Head and Pen yr Afr; the glacial meltwater features at Ceibwr **3**; the Witches Cauldron near Ceibwr **4**; the landslips on the cliffs near Cell Howell; and the strange and beautiful heath vegetation on Morfa Head **5**.

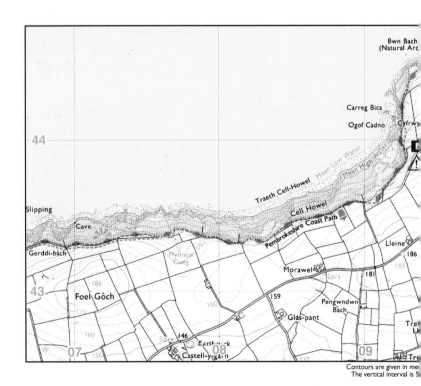

Contours are given in me
The vertical interval is 5

care. Look to the *south* of the footpath and you will see that a wide strip of land has dropped by at least 33 feet (10 metres). The fault scarps are clearly visible in the fields.

Follow the path for some 2½ miles (4 km) above the bevelled north-facing cliffs, walking for much of the time more than 500 feet (150 metres) above sea level. Down below there are a number of beaches used for breeding by Atlantic grey seals. On the flanks of the Trwyn y Bwa peninsula, look out for nesting fulmars, razorbills, guillemots and cormorants.

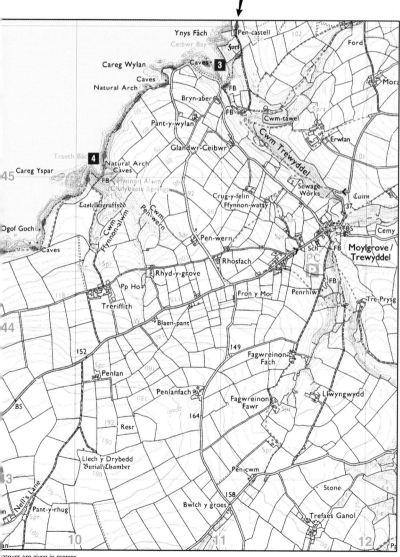

Contours are given in metres
The vertical interval is 5m

Morfa Head **5** provides glorious views across Newport Bay. As you descend southwards from the summit you pass through a rock garden of gorse and heather, one of many designated Sites of Special Scientific Interest on the Coast Path.

Traeth Mawr ('Big Beach' or Newport Sands) is one of the best beaches on the North Pembrokeshire coast. It has a good car park, surf lifesaving club, summer shop, toilets and a golf club. The Coast Path runs across the golf course to the east of the dunes **F**. Some walkers choose to follow the beach southwards and then eastwards around The Bennet. This latter route follows the north bank of the river into the sheltered estuary and is normally passable except during very high tides; at the white cottage it rejoins the Coast Path which leads to the bridge over the river.

Near Ffynnon Bryncyn there is a fine restored lime kiln. The tidal estuary hereabouts is a favourite wintering location for many waders, ducks and other birds. On the upstream side of the Iron Bridge you will see stepping stones, which may be medieval. Newport **6** is not actually on the Coast Path, but Parrog is. To reach Parrog simply continue along the wheelchair path for about half a mile (1 km), now heading westwards along the south shore of the estuary. There is a large free car park, with café and toilets; and the town also has a youth hostel.

The northern end of Newport Sands (Traeth Mawr). In this area the submerged forest can sometimes be seen

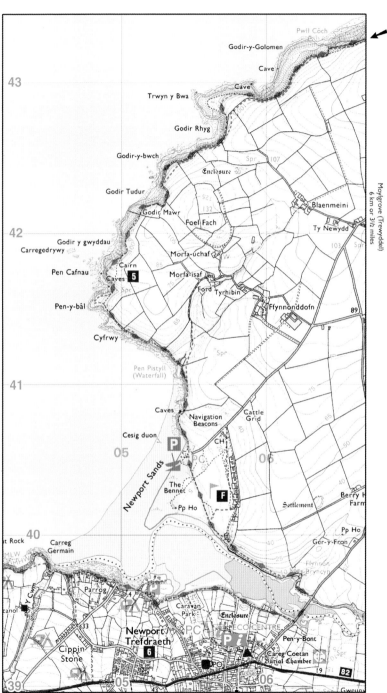

Moylgrove (Trewyddel)
6 km or 3½ miles

Pwll Côch

Godir-y-Golomen

Cave

43

Cave

Trwyn y Bwa

Cave

Godir Rhyg

Godir-y-bwch

Enclosure

107

Godir Tudur

Blaenmeini

Godir Mawr

Foel Fach

Ty Newydd

42

Godir y gwyddau

Morfa-uchaf

Carregedrywy

Cairn

Morfa-isaf

89

Pen Cafnau

Caves **5**

Ford Tyrhibin

Ffynnonddofn

Pen-y-bâl

Cyfrwy

Pen Pistyll
(Waterfall)

41

Caves

Navigation
Beacons

Cattle
Grid

Cesig duon

CH

P

05

PC

06

The
Bennet

F

Pp Ho

Settlement

Berry
Farm

40

Carreg
Germain

Pp Ho

at Rock

Ger-y-Fron

MLW

Flynnon
Bryncyn

Parrog

Caravan
Park

Enclosure

33

ECOCENTRE

Y Cwm

Newport /
Trefdraeth

PC

i

Pen-y-Bont

canol

6

P

Careg Coetan
Burial Chamber

Cippin
Stone

PO

19

82

39

05

06

Gweun

Contours are given in metres
The vertical interval is 5m

Geology

The Pembrokeshire coastline is justly famous for its magnificent cliff scenery and for its immense variety of coastal habitats. Why is there such a range of coastal types within what is geographically a very small area?

Pembrokeshire rocks belong for the most part to the Palaeozoic Era and all of them are over 300 million years old. The oldest rocks are Precambrian, and are more than 1,000 million years old. Broadly, Pembrokeshire can be divided into two structural regions. In the 'northern geological province' the rocks are of Lower Palaeozoic and Precambrian age; many are made of sea-floor sediments, although there are also igneous rocks. All these rocks were laid down before the great Caledonian mountain-building episode which culminated about 400 million years ago, creating a gigantic mountain range along the contact of the two colliding supercontinents of North America and Eurasia. The great folds (anticlines and synclines) created during this episode are responsible for the south-west to north-east 'grain' of the country in North Pembrokeshire, and around the coast the spectacular cliffs provide opportunities to examine 'slices' through these structures, with folds, faults, shattered belts and a whole host of other geological features beautifully revealed.

In North Pembrokeshire, too, the details of the coast are not due simply to the work of the sea. During the Ice Age the effects of frost, glacier ice and glacial meltwater led to the creation of many spectacular 'fossil' features. Elsewhere, ancient river valleys affect the appearance of the coastline, as at St Dogmaels, Solva and Newgale. In other places the work of wind is apparent, as at Whitesands, Poppit and Newport, where sizeable dune systems have developed in conjunction with sandy beaches.

In South Pembrokeshire the rocks are younger, all of them belonging to the Upper Palaeozoic Era. Those most commonly encountered are the red sandstones and marls of the Old Red Sandstone formation, the grey and white soluble rocks of the Carboniferous Limestone formation, and the Coal Measures of the Pembrokeshire coalfield. The great majority are sedimentary, but some igneous rocks are to be found along the southern shore of St Bride's Bay. To the south of Newgale the folds and faults were created during another episode of mountain-building called the 'Armorican' or 'Hercynian' Orogeny, which occurred immediately after the deposition of the Coal Measures. This time the grain or trend of the structure is almost east–west.

The great sweep of St Bride's Bay is the result of coastal erosion from the west of the soft rocks of the coalfield, between the hard, resistant igneous promontories tipped by Ramsey Island in the north and Skomer Island in the south. The promontory of Pen Caer owes its survival to the resistance of hard igneous rocks. The waterway of Milford Haven owes its origin to river erosion along a series of faults and outcrops of Carboniferous Limestone, with the river valley later flooded by the sea. Saundersfoot Bay owes its origin to the marine erosion of soft Coal Measures rocks along the axis of a broad syncline. Almost all of the headlands between

Marine erosion of soft shales at the base of the cliffs at Cwm-yr-Eglwys.

Strumble Head and St David's Head coincide with outcrops of hard igneous rocks, while almost all of the bays coincide with outcrops of softer shale or mudstone. On the south shore of Milford Haven, the embayments of Angle Bay and Pembroke River coincide exactly with outcrops of easily eroded limestone, whereas the narrow bay entrances have been formed through breaches of a rampart of hard Old Red Sandstone. On the magnificent Carboniferous Limestone coasts of the Castlemartin Peninsula, narrow inlets coincide with faults and bands of broken rock or 'gash breccia'; headlands often coincide with outcrops of particularly massive limestone beds.

12 ¾ miles (20.5 km)
via Cwm-yr-Eglwys and Fishguard

Ascent 2,821 feet (860 metres)
Highest point 466 feet (142 metres)

This section starts at Parrog, about half a mile (1 km) from the centre of Newport **6** and is reached via Parrog Road. The Poppit Rocket bus stops at Parrog. Newport is well served by regular bus services between Fishguard and Cardigan. There are four inns in the town as well as a number of cafés and guesthouses. The National Park Information Centre is opposite the entrance of the Long Street car park. The youth hostel is on the site of the old primary school. The National Trail between Newport and Fishguard is well marked and should present no major problems.

The Parrog is Newport's old port. Before the silting of the estuary in the late 1800s, slates, herrings and woollen fabrics were exported, and

The old port of Parrog, Newport, with the volcanic peak of Carn Ingli in the distance.

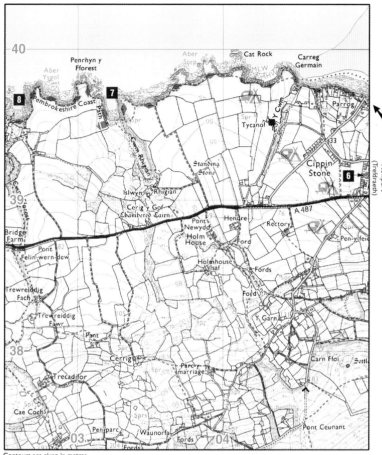

Contours are given in metres
The vertical interval is 5m

culm, limestone, wine, fruit and other luxury items were imported. There was shipbuilding and ship-repairing too. Cwm is a small beach at the western end of the Parrog, used as the focal point for Newport's annual summer regatta.

Part of the path on Parrog runs along the beach; follow the inland detour at high tide. The bay to the west of Cat Rock, like the other bays between Newport and Cwm-yr-Eglwys, has been used for the quarrying of shale slabs locally referred to as slate. The 'sea quarries' belonged

for the most part to the Llwyngwair Estate. The coast here is on an intimate scale, quite unlike that between St Dogmaels and Newport. Heading west from Parrog you reach Aberrhigian **7**, an idyllic little cove, totally unspoilt. Aberfforest **8** is very similar, with the cove occupying the seaward end of a valley. This is a popular little beach, with some sand exposed at low tide. There are reasonable conditions for launching small boats, but vehicular access is private.

The scarlet tiger moth, one of Britain's most colourful moths, can often be seen in Cwm Dewi during daylight hours.

Cwm-yr-Eglwys **9** (the Valley of the Church) is one of North Pembrokeshire's favourite beauty spots. The small settlement nestles at the eastern end of the deep valley of Cwm Dewi, well sheltered from the prevailing westerly winds. This shelter has allowed the growth of trees and shrubs of almost Mediterranean luxuriance. There is a good sandy beach, a slipway for launching boats, toilets and a small car park which can be very crowded in summer. The focal point of the settlement is the ruined church of St Brynach, destroyed by coastal erosion but once large enough to hold a congregation of 300.

There are two alternatives at this point: either carry on round Dinas Island to Dinas Head, or follow the valley path **A** to Pwllgwaelod **10**. The latter path has now been upgraded to wheelchair standard. In the woodland you should see garden warblers, chiffchaffs, willow warblers, whitethroats and blackcaps. Where there are more open conditions,

look out for the pearl-bordered fritillary among the butterflies, and also the day-flying scarlet tiger moth. Frogs, adders and grass snakes are common on the edge of the boggy land. Throughout August listen for the sound of bush crickets during the late afternoon and early evening.

The path out to Dinas Head climbs through patches of scrub and woodland, which thrive on the lee side of the headland. Needle Rock is a stack close enough to the trail to provide excellent views of nesting seabirds: herring gulls, razorbills, guillemots and shags. Ravens, jackdaws, fulmars and other gulls also nest on the mainland cliffs hereabouts. Beyond it, the long bevelled slope, terminated by sheer cliffs at the coastline proper, is reminiscent of the north-facing cliffs of Traeth Cell-Howel, east of Morfa Head. The path can be slippery here **B**. Pen y Fan is the highest point on the headland, at 466 feet (142 metres), with glorious views in all directions. Look out for grey seals down below, and out to sea you may be lucky enough to see porpoises (with triangular dorsal fins) or dolphins (with beak-like snouts and sickle-shaped dorsal fins). You may also see peregrine falcons, and gannets diving for fish offshore.

Pwllgwaelod **10**, exposed to the westerly winds, provides a striking contrast to the lush, calm environment of Cwm-yr-Eglwys. It is a popular beach none the less, with firm sand, a large car park, toilet facilities, a ruined lime kiln, and refreshments. The next stretch of coast is fascinating, with dark shale cliffs and abundant creeks, offshore stacks and little beaches down below. Pwll Gwylog is a delightful little cove.

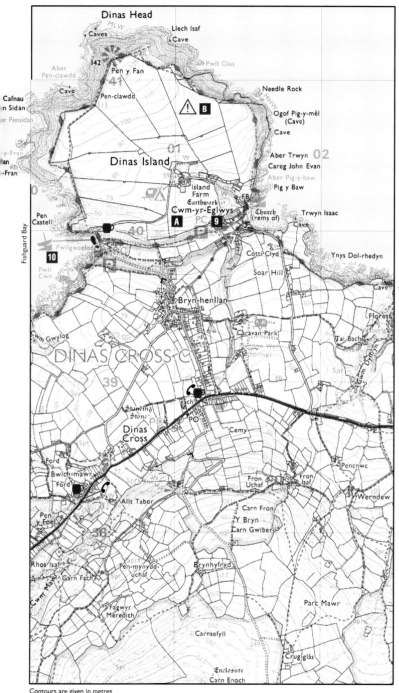

Newport (Parrog) to Goodwick Harbour (Harbour Heights)

Contours are given in metres
The vertical interval is 5m

Dinas Island (which is not an island) and the coastline to the west of Pwllgwaelod.

Hescwm (Aber Bach) **11** is a well-kept secret. The inlet is very well sheltered by the offshore stacks to the west. There is good bathing, although the beach is pebbly and rough. Access from the road is not easy, with few passing places and no parking; it is best to reach the cove by footpath. The Path heads away from the beach for a while before swinging westwards again **C**. Look out for the fingerposts on the western side.

Penrhyn still has many traces of a First World War coastal defence installation. Now the site has been transformed into a well-planned caravan park. Needle Rock (another one!) is a spectacular stack with an arch punctured through its base. Nesting bird species here, and on the cliffs adjacent to the stack, include fulmars, gulls, razorbills, guillemots and cormorants.

Continuing westwards you approach the sheltered waters of Fishguard Harbour and its 'three towns', all of which actually lie outside the National Park. On Castle Point you come across the ruins of Fishguard Fort, built in 1781 to defend the community against privateers. Lower Town (Cwm) **12** is built around the drowned western end of Cwm Gwaun, Pembrokeshire's largest and most spectacular sub-glacial meltwater channel. Cwm was Fishguard's earliest

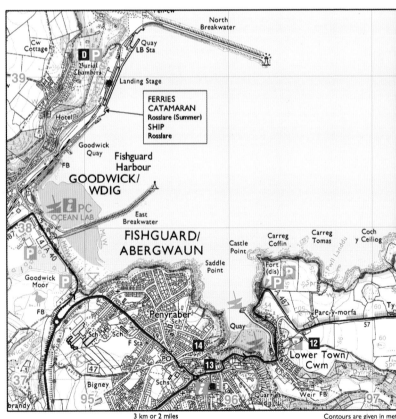

3 km or 2 miles
A40(T) Schleddau

Contours are given in met
The vertical interval is 5

settlement, earning its living from herring fishing, shipbuilding and coastal trading. From the old bridge you can either follow the main road up into the modern town of Fishguard **13**, or keep to the coast. Beyond the boat park you can follow a asphalt path towards The Slade **14**, or else (at low tide) walk along the beach. From The Slade there are a number of good paths to choose from, all following the slope along the western side of the Lower Town harbour. After passing Lampit Beach, follow the Marine Walk all the way to the picnic area and car park overlooking Goodwick (Parrog) beach. The Parrog car park is a convenient stop or start point close to garages, accommodation and cafés.

Goodwick is a large settlement clinging to a steep hillside. It owes its origins to the arrival of the railway and the creation of the port of Fishguard in Victorian times. From the car park on the Parrog follow the seaward side of the ferry complex, over the big steel footbridge. Turn right on Quay Road, then up the zigzag path, then right again through Harbour Village. Enjoy the fine views across the harbour. Car parking (free) is at the northern end of Harbour Village, but there are no other facilities here at the end of the road **D**.

Contours are given in metres
The vertical interval is 5m

The 'three towns'

Fishguard (Abergwaun) is really made up of three quite distinct communities, Lower Town (occupying the mouth of the Gwaun Valley), the modern town of Fishguard (on the higher ground to the west), and Goodwick (occupying a steep hillside above Goodwick Moor and close to the modern port).

Lower Town (or 'Cwm' as it is locally known) is the archetypal fishing village, with houses clustered close to the waterfront mainly on the eastern flank of the old harbour. The settlement survived for centuries as a small trading centre with a substantial herring fishery. There was a local shipbuilding industry, and cargoes of limestone, coal, fabrics and foodstuffs came in to balance the exports of salted herrings, woollen cloth, oats and barley. Gradually, in the late 19th century, both fishing and coastal trading declined; today the harbour is full of pleasure craft. This is one of the prettiest coastal settlements in Wales; not surprisingly, it was chosen for the film version of Dylan Thomas's *Under Milk Wood*.

The modern town was but a cluster of cottages until the early 1800s, but gradually it expanded to become the main shopping centre of North Pembrokeshire. The Market Square is the centre of affairs, with the Town Hall and The Royal Oak inn, where the surrender documents were signed following the last invasion of Britain in 1797. A wonderful tapestry, made by local people to celebrate the bicentenery of the Last Invasion, is now housed in the refurbished Town Hall.

Fishguard Harbour was constructed in the early years of the 20th century as a transatlantic passenger port, connected by rail with South Wales and London. The difficult site beneath east-facing cliffs was transformed by blasting. Two million tonnes of rock were removed, most of it built into the impressive 2,000-foot-long (610-metre) North Breakwater. The quarry floor was then used for the railway terminus, passenger station, storage sheds and quayside equipment. The work continued until 1908, when the first passenger service was inaugurated. Until the outbreak of the First World War there was hectic activity, with ships using the harbour for the Irish and transatlantic passenger services. Fishguard briefly threatened Liverpool as a transatlantic port, but the harbour could generate little economic activity locally, so its fall was as rapid as its rise. The building of the East Breakwater in 1913, intended to improve facilities, caused rapid harbour silting instead and soon it became impossible for the larger liners to tie up at the quayside. After the war the transatlantic service was not revived, but the port has remained important for the Irish service, with Stena vessels ferrying passengers, vehicles and container traffic between Fishguard and Rosslare.

Goodwick was a sleepy fishing village before the coming of the railway and the growth of the port. For many years it was, above all, a railway settlement, but many local people were employed in the port and in a local brickworks. The latter is now closed. Above the village is Harbour Village, built around 1906 to house railway and port workers. The most imposing building in Goodwick is the Fishguard Bay Hotel, overlooking the harbour. There is a pleasant sandy beach on the Parrog, and good shops and car parks. The village is now a popular holiday and boating centre, and is the service centre for the port. The sea front has been transformed by EU and other grant aid, with a marine life exhibition centre and café, and a sail training centre.

Fishguard Fort, located at the entrance to Fishguard's Lower Town harbour, was operational at the time of the French invasion of 1797.

Newport (Parrog) to Goodwick Harbour (Harbour Heights)

43

3 Goodwick Harbour (Harbour Heights) to Trefin

17 ¼ miles (27.8 km)
around Strumble Head and past Abercastle

Ascent 2,854 feet (870 metres)
Highest point 459 feet (140 metres)

The starting point **D** is about 2 miles (3 km) from the centre of Fishguard (which is well served by buses) or ½ mile (800 metres) by road from the new Fishguard railway station, now served by up to seven trains a day. There is also a regular daily town bus service which runs between Fishguard Square and Harbour Village. When you leave the Harbour Heights car park you are back to a proper footpath again. The Coast Path is both well maintained and easy to follow all the way to Trefin.

The path runs well inland at Pen Anglas, cutting off the peninsula which is famous for the columnar jointing similar to that of Fingal's Cave in the Hebrides. From the summit of Carnfathach **15** you will see typical Pen Caer scenery. Inland lies the bleak expanse of Ciliau Moor, with the volcanic crag of Garnwnda

Lower Town harbour, Fishguard, at the time of high water. It was once a busy trading and herring fishing port.

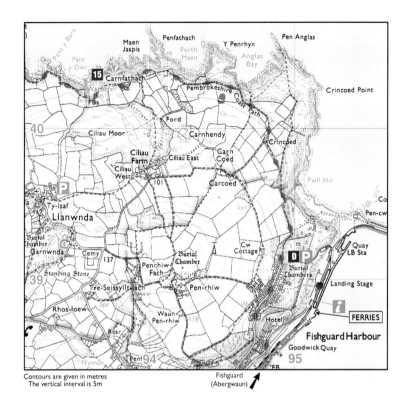

Contours are given in metres
The vertical interval is 5m

Fishguard
(Abergwaun)

beyond, smoothed during the Ice Age, like other neighbouring crags. Note the small rough fields, the stone walls, and the windblasted trees. Here and there in this harsh but beautiful environment you can see little clusters of settlement. The hamlet of Llanwnda is the main centre – half a dozen houses, an ancient green and a Celtic-style bellcote church restored in 1870.

At Cwm Felin you come unexpectedly across a most attractive and well-wooded little valley. A stream tumbles down to the shore under a canopy of lush woodland, and suddenly you hear woodland birds again. There is good shelter here in inclement weather – and it is the

Look out for . . .

. . . the location of the Last Invasion of Britain at Carregwastad **16**; Strumble Head lighthouse **17**; the famous cliffs of Pwllderi and Penbwchdy **18**; the submerged forest at Aber Mawr (if you are lucky) **19**; the pretty harbour at Abercastle.

shelter from westerly winds that enables the deciduous trees to survive and even thrive. A well-marked footpath **A** runs inland from Cwm Felin to Llanwnda, where there is some car parking space.

Carreg Goffa **16** and Carregwastad Point are the scene of the last invasion of Britain, if this is not too grand a term for it, which took place on 22 February 1797. The simple memorial stone on Carreg Goffa **16** was erected in 1897 to commemorate the landing of Colonel Tate and his 'invasion force' of 1,200 men. You can explore the peninsula before returning to the Coast Path.

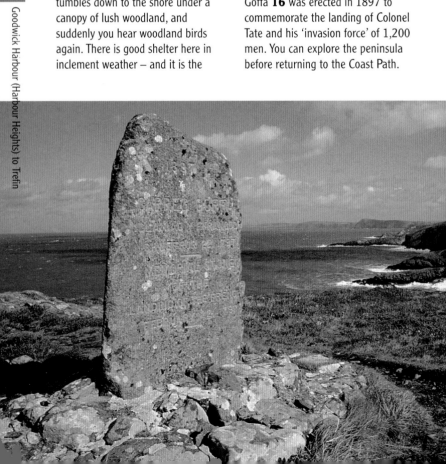

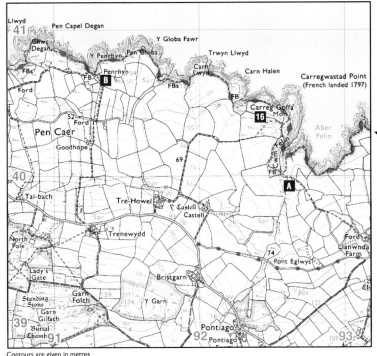

Contours are given in metres
The vertical interval is 5m

The memorial stone at Carreg Goffa, erected to commemorate the 'Last Invasion of Britain' in 1797.

To the west of Pen Globa the path passes through an area of bluish-green dolerite outcrops, springy turf and gorse bushes. Abundant lichens and spring flowers make this a most colourful and fascinating stretch of the path. Penrhyn is an idyllic spot, with a lonely cottage located adjacent to the footpath. The pretty, whitewashed building sits on a grassy bank that runs down to a narrow creek. There are three possible routes here **B**. One runs southwards to Goodhope and Trenewydd; a second follows the track westwards to Tresinwen; and the third, on the clifftop, is the National Trail.

The spectacular cliffs at Pwll Deri, with the crags of Garn Fawr on the skyline.

The trail follows a beautiful stretch of coast between Carreg Onnen Bay and Pen Brush, about 1½ miles (2 km) away, weaving in and out of a range of little hillocks of volcanic rock, all rounded and smoothed by ice action. Pwll Arian (loosely translated, Silver Cove or Treasure Cove) is a delightful spot where a small valley runs down to the sea. Banks of springy turf, reed beds and copses of bushes make this an ideal location for a picnic. As you walk south-eastwards from Pen Brush there is shelter in old Ministry of Defence buildings both above and below the footpath. Porth Maenmelyn is a wild little cove. Dinas Mawr is an Iron Age promontory fort defended by a double embankment. Keep an eye open for choughs hereabouts, and also for breeding seals in the late autumn. Pwllderi Youth Hostel is nearby.

Strumble Head **17** is a glorious, wild stretch of coast, savagely impressive during storm conditions. Because of its easy access by road, it is also popular with naturalists. The restored Ministry of Defence building close to the car park provides birdwatchers with some shelter. This is an immensely popular spot among 'twitchers' who wish to observe the spring and autumn bird migrations at close quarters. Below the observation post there are some classic exposures of pillow lavas. The pillow-shaped masses are the result of the very rapid cooling of volcanic lavas extruded on to the sea floor during submarine eruptions about 450 million years ago. A little further to the west the lighthouse on the island of Ynys Meicel is sometimes accessible via a small footbridge. It is not manned, and is therefore not normally open to the public.

Pwll Deri **18** is one of Pembrokeshire's favourite beauty spots, eroded by the sea along soft shales and bounded to the north by a great mass of dolerites and other hard volcanic rocks. These igneous rocks have been resistant to marine erosion, and remain as wave-swept offshore islands, stacks and skerries, while the softer sedimentary rocks have been eroded away. On its south side the bay is bordered by the great rampart of cliffs running for 1¼ miles (2 km) south-westwards towards Penbwchdy. In places these cliffs are over 450 feet (137 metres) high, providing Pwll Deri Youth Hostel (opened in 1957) with the most exposed and spectacular site of all the hostels in Pembrokeshire. After climbing up to the road **C**, pass the memorial stone and small car parking area before rejoining the footpath proper to head south-west towards Carn Ogof.

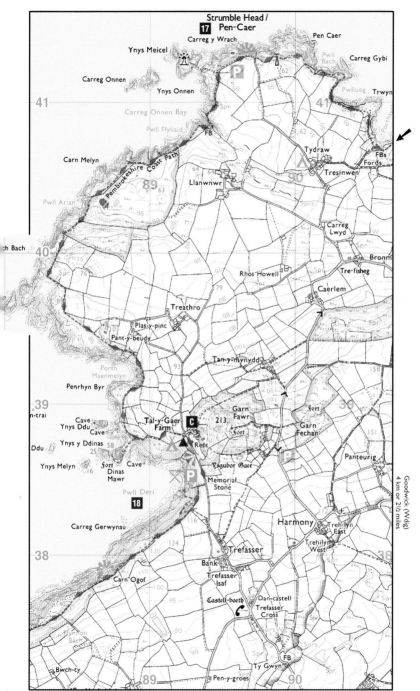

Contours are given in metres
The vertical interval is 5m

The treeless, windswept landscape of Pencaer, from the summit of Garn Fawr. Strumble Head lighthouse is in the distance.

50

Goodwick Harbour (Harbour Heights) 165 m

If you look inland from Penbwchdy towards the village of St Nicholas, you will be able to see a strange hilltop structure on the skyline. This is 'Green One', the civil aircraft homing beacon used by transatlantic traffic. From the footpath at Penbwchdy, looking westwards towards the tip of the peninsula, you can also see a circular, dry stone structure, which was once a shepherd's shelter.

Now continue to Pwllcrochan, an attractive small bay cut into contorted and broken soft sedimentary rocks, with some sand exposed at low tide. Access is dangerous – do not try to scramble down to the beach near the stream. Further south, Aber Bach is a pretty bay with a massive storm beach that has impounded a small stream in the valley. If this stream is in spate, you can cross the valley via an alternative waymarked route. Notice the little ruined boathouse

The 'kelp forest' at Aber Mawr, exposed only at times of low water spring tides.

Aber Mawr **19** has a wide sandy beach backed by an impressive storm beach of pebbles. Access is good, but there is no car park, and only limited roadside parking on a grassy verge. Aber Mawr is probably the most important Ice Age site in Pembrokeshire. The cliffs of unconsolidated sediments at the north end of the bay reveal a sequence of deposits from the last glacial episode, while the organic deposits on the floor of the valley behind the storm beach span the last 14,000 years or so. The submerged forest is occasionally exposed through the sandy beach following winter storms. The old roadway that once connected the two sides of the bay has gradually been eroded away, because the coast has retreated inland by about 130 feet (40 metres). Descend to the storm beach and continue to the southern end of the bay, where the Trail has been rerouted due to erosion.

In the lee of Penmorfa the cliffs are extremely well protected from the prevailing westerlies and south-westerlies. Note that the cliff profiles are much gentler, affording easy access to the sea in many places. In contrast, the west-facing cliffs across the bay are steep and constantly battered by storm waves. On the peninsula, Castell-coch is an Iron Age promontory fort with ditches and double embankments, and a zig-zag central entrance designed to resist direct attack. There are lovely views from the outer part of Trwyn Llwynog peninsula. Continue to Aber Mochyn ('the Bay of the Pig'). Be careful of clifftop instability here – you will see much evidence of subsidence, rockfalls and rotational slips in the cliff face **D**.

On the western side of Pwllstrodur **E** there is more evidence of coastal instability.

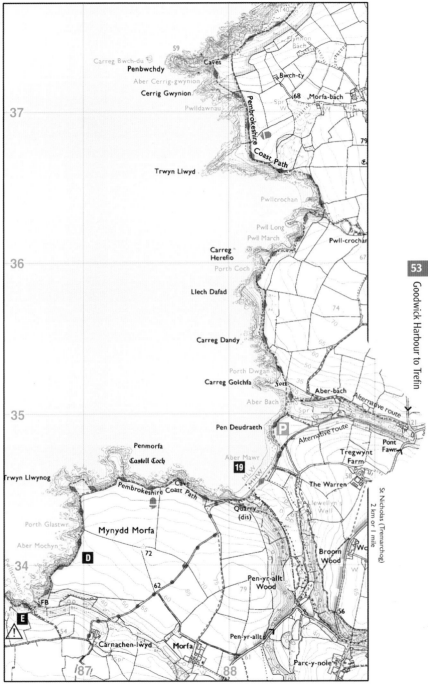

Penbwchdy
Carreg Bwch-du
Caves
Aber Cerrig-gwynion
Cerrig Gwynion
Pwlldawnau
59
Bwch-ty
68 Morfa-bach
Spr W
79
Pembrokeshire Coast Path
37
Trwyn Llwyd
Pwllcrochan
Pwll Long
Pwll March
Pwll-crochan
67
Carreg Herefio
Porth Coch
36
Llech Dafad
74
70
Carreg Dandy
65
60
50
Porth Dwgan
Carreg Golchfa
Sort
35
Aber-bach
Alternative route
Aber Bach
Spr
21
Pen Deudraeth
P
Alternative route
Pont Fawr
Penmorfa
Tregwynt Farm
Castell Coch
Aber Mawr
Trwyn Llwynog
Pembrokeshire Coast Path
Cave
The Warren
58
Llewellyn's Well
Porth Glastwr
Quarry (dis)
19
MLW
MHW
Mynydd Morfa
Broom Wood
Wo
Aber Mochyn
D
72
Pen-yr-allt Wood
34
62
79
56
FB
60
65
E
⚠
54
Carnachen-lwyd
Morfa
Pen-yr-allt
Parc-y-nole
87
88

St. Nicholas (Tremarchog)
2 km or 1 mile

Contours are given in metres
The vertical interval is 5m

You soon see a most impressive field wall, labelled by the weary builder 'The Great Wall of China'. Then, a further half-mile to the west, you come upon Abercastle. This is a delightful creek – one of the multitude of little harbours on the Pembrokeshire coast used by trading vessels until well into the 20th century. There is a cluster of houses and cottages around the head of the inlet, and a number of other typical features – an old granary (roofless and derelict), two fine bollards (made of old cannons embedded in the turf), a lime kiln and the remains of a lime-burner's cottage.

Carreg Samson cromlech (burial chamber) **20** is accessible even though it is some way off the trail. The capstone is over 16 feet (5 metres) long and almost 10 feet (3 metres) wide, resting on three of the six uprights. The burial chamber was built about 5,000 years ago; it was probably used for at least 100 different burials by the Neolithic tribe in whose territory it lay.

Further west, Pen Castell-coch is a delightful peninsula, projecting far out from the coast and connected to the mainland by a narrow neck. It is a splendid spot for a picnic – springy turf, flowers in spring, skylarks and seabirds, and wonderful coastal views to the south-west. There is rapid coastal erosion beyond the peninsula. Note the rock pinnacles, rockfalls, fault scarps and cliff-face slumps. To the south, Pwll Llong is a small bay contained by high cliffs and accessible via a steep path, but the beach is rocky and pebbly. Many fulmars nest hereabouts. There is footpath access to Trefin and the youth hostel from the National Trail just to the east of Trwyn Llwyd **F**.

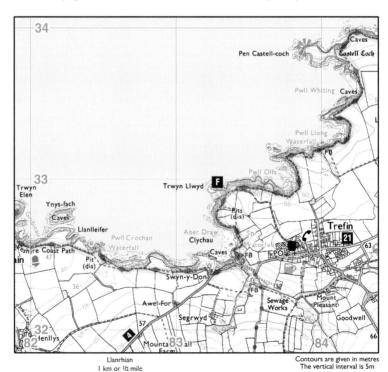

Llanrhian
1 km or ½ mile

Contours are given in metres
The vertical interval is 5m

Aber Draw (Aber Felin) is the beach for Trefin **21**. It is too rocky and exposed ever to have played much part in coastal trading, but there is a sandy beach at low water. The ruined Melin Trefin was one of the multitude of little corn mills that served the farming community in the 19th century. You can also reach Trefin by bearing left up the hill when you get to the tarmac road. It is the largest of the coastal villages between St David's and Goodwick. One of the early palaces of the Bishop of St David's was built here, but is now lost without trace. Although just off the National Trail, Trefin is a good point for stopping or starting a walk, being served by an inn and by a regular daily bus service between St David's and Fishguard. The Strumble Shuttle bus also stops here, and there is a refurbished hostel in the village.

55

Millstones left behind in the ruins of Melin Trefin, adjacent to the Coast Path.

Harbour (Harbour Heights) to Trefin

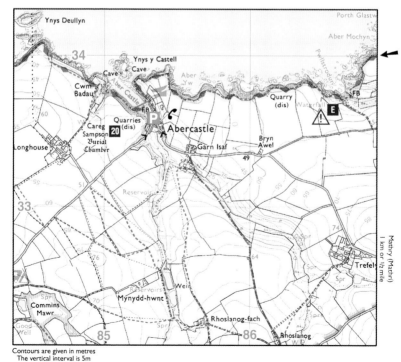

Mathry (Mathri)
1 km or ½ mile

Contours are given in metres
The vertical interval is 5m

The spectacular cliffed rampart of Penbwchdy, with the coastline of the St David's Peninsula beyond.

The Celts and their forts

The Celtic immigrant tribes who moved into Pembrokeshire about 2,600 years ago made a more dramatic and lasting impact upon the landscape than any of their predecessors. They were more ferocious, more organised, and more practised in the arts of war and peace than the Bronze Age settlers already in residence, and as the centuries passed they tamed large parts of the Pembrokeshire wilderness by clearing the forest, building villages and fortifications, and introducing many new agricultural practices. They sowed and harvested new crops, kept domesticated animals, and enclosed fields and paddocks with drystone walls. They also rode horses, which made them fearsome warriors, and they had armour and weapons far in advance of anything used by the Bronze Age people.

It is often said that whereas the Bronze Age people practised the arts of peace, the Iron Age invaders practised the arts of war. Things were certainly not that simple, but such was the scale of the immigration into western Britain that inter-tribal and even inter-family feuding must have become a way of life, as groups of all sizes jostled for the best land, the best water supplies, and the best-defended sites.

The Iron Age hill fort or promontory fort is the most striking of all the prehistoric features to be found in Wales, and in Pembrokeshire such forts are particularly numerous. Earth ramparts and ditches appear with almost predictable regularity on hill summits, river valley spurs, and – of most interest to those walking the National Trail – on promontories all the way round the coast. Almost every self-respecting headland has its promontory fort, and the features of earth and stone provide an insight into the evolution of defensive strategies as the Iron Age ran its course. The earliest forts were protected only by single-curved banks and ditches, but by 100 BC double, triple and even quadruple embankments and ditches were common, with complicated entrance passages and devices designed to repel boarders. Many embankments were faced with stone; sometimes these were over 15 feet (4.5 metres) high, and sometimes they bristled with pointed stakes. No doubt the defenders knew all about arrows, spears, boulders and boiling water too. Sometimes the enclosed areas were small, and used only as last-ditch defensive positions (which is where the phrase probably comes from); but other fortified sites enclosed areas of land large enough to enable a family group and its animals to sit out a prolonged siege.

Some of the promontory forts contain traces of Iron Age hut circles (as on St David's Head), and here and there you can see traces of Iron Age field boundaries. The largest of all the coastal defended sites is the Deer Park at Martin's Haven, but those who feel like a short detour from the trail can climb Garn Fawr (close to Pwll Deri) or Carn Ingli (close to Newport) for a glimpse of a genuine hill summit settlement with all its trappings.

At Castell Henllys, near Eglwyswrw, an Iron Age fort has been excavated and developed by the National Park Authority as an educational resource. Reconstructed round houses provide fascinating insights into the lives of the original inhabitants.

4 Trefin to Whitesands Bay

11¼ miles (18 km)
via Porth-gain and Abereiddi

Ascent 1,935 feet (590 metres)
Highest point 394 feet (120 metres)

Starting from Trefin, follow the road westwards to Aber Draw beach and climb up the hill on the far side of the valley. Where signposted, turn right, off the road.

Follow the farm track **A** west across the fields. Note the volcanic boulders collected by generations of farmers from the fields. After passing the waterfall in Pwll Crochan Bay, stick to the footpath; small

ploughed fields intervene between the path and the coastline. After making contact with the coast again, you come to a choice of routes **B**. Either take the shortcut to Porthgain **22** or follow the coast via Trwyn Elen. Porth-gain 22 is one of the most popular places on the north Pembrokeshire coast, and it can be very crowded in summer. It is a

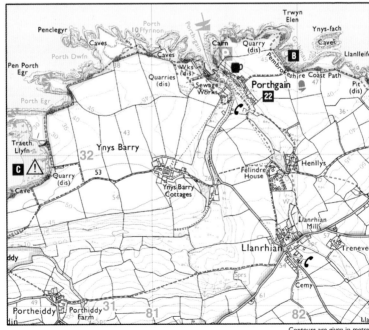

Contours are given in metres
The vertical interval is 5m

fascinating old port, heavy with the atmosphere of Pembrokeshire's short-lived Industrial Revolution. The little harbour was used in the period 1837–1931 for the export of roadstone, slates and bricks. Note the old brickworks (now restored) and the massive bins that held the crushed stone. Walk out along the western edge of the harbour and climb the steps near the old pilot house. On the cliff tops look for traces of Pentop quarrymen's row, the slate/shale quarry and tramway cutting, trackbeds galore, dust and crushed stone, the remains of the stone-crushing plant, the old weighbridge, water tank and engine shed, spoil tips of slate rubble, and the small fields used by the eight horses that pulled the tramway trucks prior to 1909.

Out towards Penclegyr you will see the vast dolerite quarry with two levels and the cable-worked incline (to the bottom level), the railway cutting (to the upper level), the winding house and smithy remains, connected by 'the Jerusalem Road' to the yard, with loops and loco shed further east. There is a rutted track to Traeth Llyfn and there may well have been a short-lived tramway here around 1880, connecting the Penclegyr stone quarry with Abereiddy.

Traeth Llyfn is an attractive sandy beach backed by dark shale cliffs. It is somewhat claustrophobic, but it is a popular bathing beach. Beware of dangerous cliffs and being cut off by a rising tide when you are on the left-hand side of the beach **C**. Access is via steel steps. Further to the west, you can enjoy the lovely views from the summit

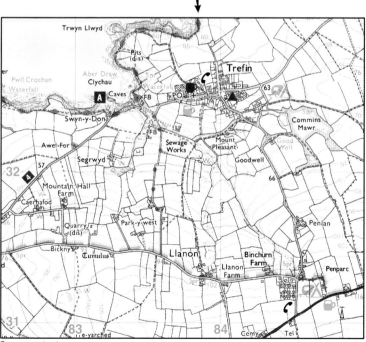

Contours are given in metres
The vertical interval is 5m

Cove with a small pebbly beach to the west of the village of Trefin.

of Carn Lwyd, a crag of the Ordovician volcanic rock which runs out to the headland of Trwyncastell. The stone tower on the headland may be an 18th-century 'pharos' tower rather than a harbour entrance marker.

Abereiddy Slate Quarry **23**, operational from about 1830 to 1904, produced slate of poor quality. Dressed slates were taken in horse-drawn trucks along the tramway to a slate yard near Barry Island Farm, and thence to Porthgain for shipment. Buildings still visible at Abereiddy Quarry include dressing sheds, the engine house (on the ledge above the flooded quarry called the Blue Lagoon), the quarrymen's row, the round powder store, and the buttressed quarry manager's house. The bay is popular

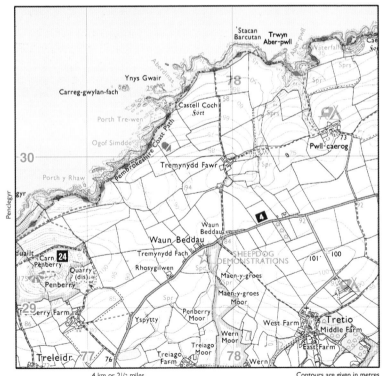

4 km or 2½ miles
B4330 St David's (Tyddewi)

Contours are given in metres
The vertical interval is 5m

with visitors because the free car park gives direct access to the black sandy beach. The cluster of simple cottages, lime kiln and industrial relics combine to make this a favourite spot with artists. There are no facilities apart from a toilet block and an occasional ice-cream van.

From Abereiddy follow the road southwards until a fingerpost directs you back to the Coast Path. Soon you come to Caerau, a most impressive complex of three Iron Age forts, with well-preserved ditches, embankments and stone-faced ramparts. After a mile or so the Iron Age theme continues

when you encounter yet another Castell Coch, set in the midst of wild and chaotic cliff scenery, with a double ditch and embankment across the headland.

From Porth y Rhaw onwards you are walking on hard igneous rocks. Note the contrast in appearance between the cliffs to the west and the soft crumbly cliffs to the north-east. Above Penclegyr the path climbs up quite steeply on the flank of Carn Penberry (Penbiri) **24**. This was an island in Pliocene times, when the gently undulating platform of the St David's peninsula was being fashioned by wave action. Near the

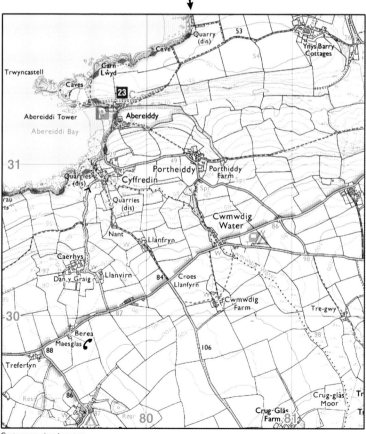

Contours are given in metres
The vertical interval is 5m

point where the path splits **D** you will see a veritable rock garden with gorse and many other flowering species at their best in early summer. This is reputed to be the spot where Ffos y Mynach (the Monk's Dyke) reaches the coast.

Most of the coast to the west of Penberry is owned by the National Trust. It is worth protecting, with complicated geology, fine cliffs, the hill masses of Carnedd-lleithr, Carn Perfedd and Carn Treliwyd to the south, and carpets of flowers in early summer. From the footpath you will catch glimpses of the 'deserted village' of Maes-y-mynydd, complete with ruined buildings, stone-walled fields and other enclosures. The village is probably medieval, but may go back to the Iron Age.

Beyond the inlet of Gesail-fawr and the peninsula of Penllechwen, the Coast Path is

difficult to discern, but it matters not – you can wander about more or less at will, as this is still National Trust land. This is another fabulous stretch for wild flowers. The cliffs are very popular with climbers. As you wander south-westwards through this heathery rock garden, look across the valley towards the rocky hill of Carn Llidi; there is hardly a trace of a man-made feature in the landscape, and it is easy to feel yourself transported back in time. But look carefully and you will see that on both sides of the valley there are signs of low and irregular Iron Age field boundaries.

As you approach the bleak peninsula of St David's Head, look out for Coetan Arthur **25**, a somewhat crude Neolithic burial chamber dating back to about 3,500 BC. A large flat capstone is supported at one end by a single vertical pillar and at the other

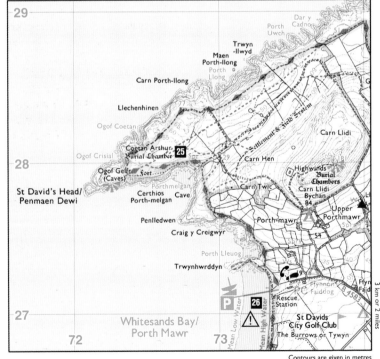

Contours are given in metres
The vertical interval is 5m

B4583 St. David's (Tyddewi)
3 km or 2 miles

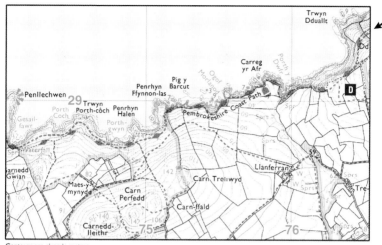

Contours are given in metres
The vertical interval is 5m

end rests on the ground. Around the cromlech is a largely unaltered Ice Age landscape, with glaciated slabs and massive erratic boulders. But look closer, and you will see the hand of prehistoric man. Clawdd-y-Milwyr (the Warrior's Dyke) is a magnificent defensive line of two ramparts and three ditches almost at the tip of the peninsula. The main drystone wall was originally 15 feet (4.5 metres) high. Within the defended area there are eight Iron Age hut circles, all clearly visible.

Once you have rounded the peninsula, Porthmelgan is a pleasant sandy beach,

easily accessible from Whitesands Bay via the Path. Take great care on this popular, heavily used section of cliff-top path.

At Whitesands **26** there is a good car park (not free), but because this is the most popular beach on the St David's Peninsula you may find it congested on a fine summer's day. However, there is a frequent bus service from St David's. Adjacent to the car park you will find toilets and a seasonal shop. The nearest accommodation is at the youth hostel on the south side of Carn Llidi (about half a mile from the beach).

Coetan Arthur, a sub-megalithic 'earthfast' tomb of Neolithic age, near the tip of St David's Head.

The heyday of the little ports

In this peninsula the little ports and harbours were vital for the smooth operation of the local economy. Until the building of good roads, and until the arrival of the railway in the mid-19th century, Pembrokeshire's contacts with the outside world were almost all by sea. Just as the early immigrants arrived by sea, the western seaways in general, and the Celtic seaways in particular, kept trading and cultural contacts alive for well over 1,000 years. The Vikings, although they caused a certain amount of local trouble, heralded the dawn of an era of sea trading. They used larger and more seaworthy vessels than anything seen before around these coasts. The Normans and their followers further developed trading links, and these were maintained until the early part of the present century.

The narrow and sheltered harbour of Solva, on the south side of the St David's Peninsula, was formed by the flooding of an old glacial meltwater channel.

Because each little creek or inlet served its own small community there was little or no trading competition in the early centuries; every creek or cove with reasonable shelter became the base for small sailing vessels and even for shipbuilding operations. Lime kilns appeared all around the coastline, sometimes adjacent to quite exposed beaches where the landing of limestone and coal must have been hazardous, to say the least. Among the main shipbuilding centres were Newport, St Dogmaels, Solva, Dale and Angle. Fishguard, Pembroke, Haverfordwest and Tenby developed as sizeable trading centres and by 1600 there were many wealthy merchants. The main items of coastal trade were coal, corn, hides, raw wool and woollen cloth, timber and slate shipped out; and luxury goods, wine, fruit, spices, pitch and fine cloths shipped in. The growth of the herring fishery went hand-in-hand with the rise of Fishguard and Tenby, and in the sheltered waters of Milford Haven the oyster and cockle fishery was of great importance to Llangwm, Lawrenny and Angle.

In the 17th and 18th centuries smuggling and piracy became popular local activities, and some of the wealthy local gentry became, very mysteriously, even wealthier. The main cargoes in smuggled goods were wine, salt and tobacco, but gold, silver, spices, silks and other luxury goods appeared from time to time in the most unlikely places.

The scale of local trade was most impressive in the period 1550–1850. For example, in 1680 there were no fewer than 793 registered shipping movements in and out of Pembrokeshire ports, and goodness knows how many

unregistered ones. In the later part of this period, stone, slate and coal began to figure prominently in coastal trading, and ports such as Porthgain, Newport, Lawrenny, Nolton and Saundersfoot began to specialise in the handling of mineral cargoes. But, as with general trading activities, the coming of the roads and railways opened up the interior of Pembrokeshire, and with the arrival of the traction engine and then the internal combustion engine it became impossible for the small trading vessels based in the small ports to compete. By the end of the First World War most of the sailing vessels and barges had been sold, or were laid up as rotting hulks. Now there are only the derelict stone quays, the bollards, the little warehouses and the coastal lime kilns to remind us of this fascinating episode in Pembrokeshire history.

5 Whitesands Bay to Solva

12 miles (19.3 km)

taking in Port Clais and St Non's Bay

Ascent 1,575 feet (480 metres)

Highest point 213 feet (65 metres)

Whitesands Bay **26** can be reached quite easily from St David's. The Celtic Coaster bus serves Whitesands from the city centre, or if you take the road north-west from the cathedral car park you will reach the bay after a walk of 1½ miles (2.5 km). Then follow the Coast Path, which is so well marked all the way to Solva that instead of concentrating on finding your way you can relax and enjoy the cliff scenery, which is quite magnificent. As you walk take note of the excellent National Trust management work.

The bay (Porth Mawr) has one of Pembrokeshire's finest sandy beaches. There are good surfing and wind-surfing conditions. But bathers should beware of a dangerous undertow and currents near Trwynhwrddyn Headland. The little Celtic chapel shown on the map has disappeared without trace. At low tide it is possible to walk southwards on the beach, but be sure to rejoin the Coast Path south of The Burrows before the cliffs start to rise along the shoreline.

Most of the rocks along this stretch of coast are of Cambrian age – they are predominantly greenish sandstones. But south of Ogofgolchfa there are exposures of the beautiful Cambrian basal conglomerate near the path. This strange rock looks like an ornamental concrete made for a rock garden, packed as it is with rounded cobbles and pebbles of purple, red and white quartzite, jasper and ash derived from the nearby Precambrian volcanic rocks. The conglomerate was formed about 570 million years ago.

The stretch from Porthselau to St Justinian's is one of the least demanding cliff walks on the trail. After rounding Point St John there are lovely views across the sound to Ramsey Island **27** (see partial map on page 70).

St Justinian's (Porthstinian) **28** is easily reached by road from St David's and there is limited car parking near the lifeboat station. The anchorage is very exposed, but it is used none the less by the Ramsey Island passenger boats, a few fishing boats and assorted pleasure craft. The lifeboat station was built in 1911–12. A little way to the south, Castell Heinif is one of the more impressive Iron Age forts, with a double embankment and a deeply excavated ditch. At the sheltered anchorage of Carn ar Wig note the old quay and winding-gear. This was the anchorage for the boats belonging to the Ramsey Island Farm.

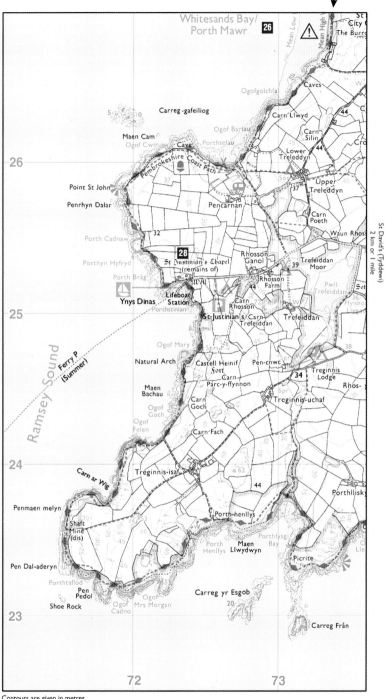

Whitesands Bay/
Porth Mawr

26

St
City
The Burr

Caves

Ogofgolchfa

Carn Llwyd

Carn
Silin

44

Cro

Carreg -gafeiliog

Maen Cam

Ogof Cwm

Caves

Porthselau

Ogof Bariau

Lower
Treleddyn

44

26

Pembrokeshire Coast Path

Point St John

Penrhyn Dalar

Pencarnan

Upper
Treleddyn

37

Carn
Poeth

Waun Rhoss

Porth Cadnaw

32

St David's (Tyddewi)
2 km or 1 mile

Porthyn Hyfryd

28

St Justinian's Chapel
(remains of)

Rhosson
Ganol

Trefeiddan
Moor

39

Porth Brâg

Well

Rhosson
Farm

44

Pwll
Trefeiddan

Ynys Dinas

Lifeboat
Station

Carn
Rhosson

Porthstinian

St Justinian's/Carn
Trefeiddan

Trefeiddan

25

38

Ogof Mary

Natural Arch

Castell Heinif
Fort

Carn
Parc-y-ffynnon

Pen-cnwc

Treginnis
Lodge

34

Rhos-

Maen
Bachau

Ogof
Goch

Carn
Goch

Treginnis-uchaf

Ferry P
(Summer)

Ramsey Sound

Ogof
Felen

Carn-Fach

24

Carn ar Wig

Treginnis-isaf

63

44

Porthllisk

Penmaen melyn

Shaft
Mine
(dis)

Porth-henllys

Pen Dal-aderyn

Porthtaflod

Porth
Henllys

Maen
Llwydwyn

Porthlysg
Bay

Picrite

Lle

Pen
Pedol

Ogof
Mrs Morgan

Carreg yr Esgob

Shoe Rock

Ogof
Cadno

20

Carreg Frân

23

72

73

Contours are given in metres
The vertical interval is 5m

The old farmhouse on Ramsey Island. Across the sound, we can see the mainland and the rocky crags that dominate the landscape.

The Bitches are a series of jagged rocks running out into the narrowest part of Ramsey Sound. The Great Bitch, closest to Ramsey, is split apart and also has a natural arch. From the mainland you can see (and hear!) the tide rushing through The Bitches; the tidal stream reaches a speed of 7 knots at times. This part of the Sound is a fearsome one for seafarers, and The Bitches have claimed many vessels.

Continuing southwards past Penmaen melyn, look out for the huge glacial erratic boulder, 14 feet (4.25 metres) long and 8 feet (2.4 metres) high, one of the most impressive to be seen anywhere on the trail. A little further on, the Ramsey Sound copper mine **29** is a somewhat mysterious relic. The mine was worked intermittently during the 19th century, and was referred to by the locals as 'Cuba'. It was the scene of a fatal accident in 1883

when a workman fell from a basket in the shaft. The men operating the winch were charged with manslaughter but acquitted after a trial at the Mathry Sessions. The mine was subsequently closed. Note the old shaft (nowadays fenced off), the piles of mine waste, and the remains of a crude building.

From Pen Dal-aderyn there are superb views of the cliff scenery on the south side of Ramsey Island **27**. Walking eastwards now, you come to Porthlysgi after about a mile (1.5 km). The bay is named after Lysgi, a wicked Irish chieftain. This is not a good bathing beach; hardly any sand is exposed, even at low tide. Edible sea kale grows near the stream mouth. Close to the old track there are the ruins of the first St David's lifeboat station, used for housing the *Augusta* (1869–85).

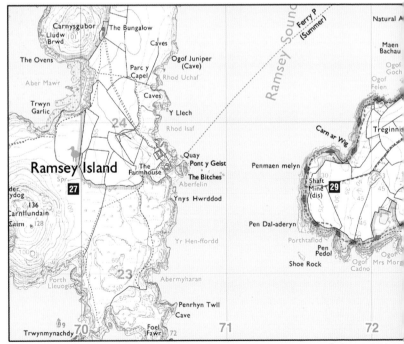

Porth Clais **30** has always been the harbour for the city of St David's, used by saints, disciples and pilgrims during the Age of the Saints, and by little trading vessels during the centuries that followed. The small breakwater may date from Norman times, but it was extensively restored in 1722. At the head of the creek you will see two stone quarries, four lime kilns (three of them very carefully restored) and the old trading quays. The car park, seasonal café and toilets are on the site of the old gasworks which provided town gas to the village-city until 1950. Although the inner part of the creek dries completely at low tide, Porth Clais still has a few fishing boats and is popular with the owners of pleasure craft.

Flowering sea kale – one of the plants frequently encountered along the Coast Path.

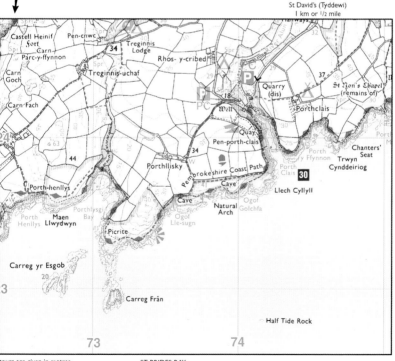

ST BRIDES BAY

Rock climbing is a popular activity near Porth Clais, where there are many near-vertical rock slabs made of hard Cambrian sandstone.

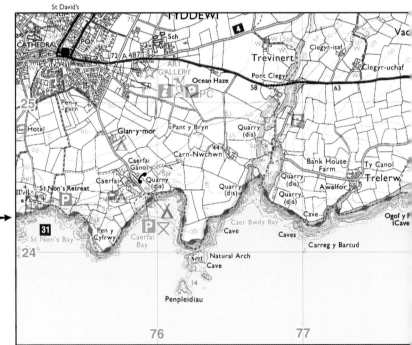

St Non's Bay **31** is a place of peace, named after the mother of St David. The patron saint was born here during a great storm about AD 462, and the ruined chapel marks the spot. The holy well of St Non was a famous healing well, especially renowned for curing eye diseases. St Non's Retreat was built by the Passionist Fathers in 1929, and the present St Non's Chapel was built (in the authentic early-Celtic style) in 1934, using stones from the ruins of nearby Whitewell Priory.

Caerfai Bay has a sheltered sandy beach, justifiably popular with visitors to St David's and easily reached by car. Some of the red and purple sandstone used for St David's Cathedral was taken from the quarries below the car park. There is good access to the beach. To the east, Penpleidiau is a magnificent Iron Age fort, with four defensive embankments and ditches. Caer Bwdy Bay is an attractive small bay, accessible from the main road at Pont Clegyr. Adjacent to the footpath you will see a massive and unusual square lime kiln as well as the remains of an old corn mill.

At Trelerw you can see a typical small Celtic settlement cluster. Hamlets like this were scattered all over the St David's peninsula; some of them probably date back to the Iron Age. At Ogof y Ffos you pass the southern end of Ffos y Mynach.

Porth y Rhaw is at the mouth of another meltwater channel and there are steep gradients on both sides of the valley **A**. At the head of the valley there were nine holy wells, much visited by the sick in the medieval period.

After a further half-mile or so the path swings northwards as you approach Solva **32**. Walk straight on into Upper Solva or descend to the quayside by following the National Trail signs.

Solva Harbour is a ria – the drowned outer portion of a complex meltwater channel that extends right into the heart of the St David's peninsula. In the 1300s it was a small port and it developed as the main trading centre on the coasts of St Bride's Bay. In the 1770s the first Smalls lighthouse was conceived and built at Solva, and shipped out to the lethal Smalls rocks, 22 miles (35 km) offshore. Solva was the main lime-burning centre for the St David's peninsula, and in Victorian times there were 10 kilns in operation. The group of kilns on the flank of the Gribin **33**, near the car park, is worth examining. On the Gribin, notice the promontory fort at the tip of the peninsula and traces of a large settlement at its inland end.

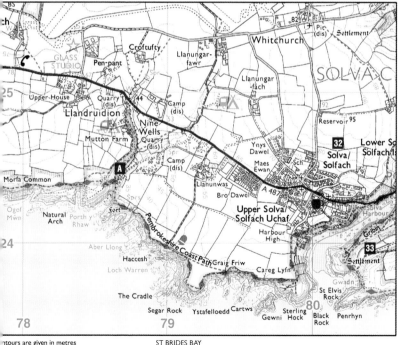

ST BRIDES BAY

St David and the Age of the Saints

The centuries that followed the departure of the Romans from Britain are generally referred to as the Dark Ages. But here in West Wales there was a thriving Christian community involved in a great flowering of civilisation. The 'Age of the Saints' spread across the western seaways to incorporate Ireland, the Isle of Man, North Wales, Pembrokeshire and Cornwall. There was a constant traffic in ideas, and the people of this western world were united by language, religion and art.

St David was one of the key figures of this period, although we must recognise that he was but one of many hundreds of devout and ascetic men who gave their lives to God as missionaries or monks in this far-flung corner of the Christian world. David was born at St Non's, baptised at Porth Clais, and educated near the little city that now bears his name. He spent most of his missionary life far away from his home area in other parts of the Celtic world, but in his old age returned to

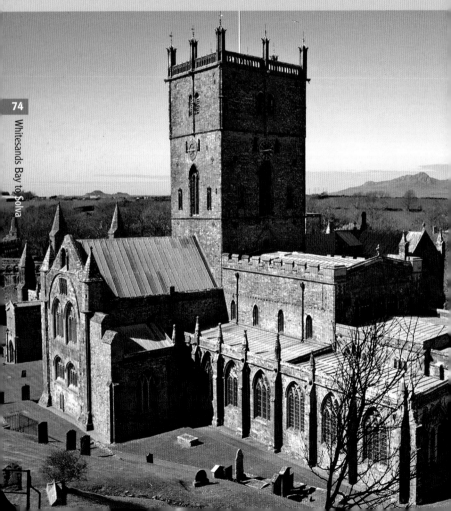

be revered as a great Christian leader. Monks and disciples travelled to his *llan* (monastic settlement) from other parts of Wales, from Brittany, Cornwall and Ireland. After his death in AD 588 his cult grew in strength; over 100 churches and monasteries were established in his name and pilgrims began to visit the little settlement in increasing numbers. Other sites of pilgrimage in the St David's peninsula included St Non's, Nine Wells, St Justinian's and Porthmawr (Whitesands) – all having strong associations with the patron saint.

The shrine at St Non's is reputed to be the place where Dewi Sant (Saint David) was born.

The cathedral of St David, the patron saint of Wales. It is built on a valley floor, and the settling of the sediments has given the nave an alarming slope . . .

The cathedral of St David is, of course, the focal point of the little city, and is easily reached from the Coast Path. It nestles in the secluded valley of the River Alun, its tower just visible from the open coast. The present building is some way from the original monastic settlement and it is at least the fourth cathedral on this site, three earlier ones having been destroyed by the Vikings. The current structure was commenced in 1180, but it took several centuries of work under a succession of bishops to give it its present form. Adjacent to the cathedral itself are the buildings of St Mary's College and the remains of the magnificent Bishop's Palace, built by Bishop Gower in 1328–47. The old bell tower has been restored and is now open to the public.

12 miles (19.3 km)

passing Newgale, Nolton Haven and Broad Haven

Ascent 2,231 feet (680 metres)
Highest point 279 feet (85 metres)

Solva is well served by a daily bus service linking St David's, Fishguard and Haverfordwest, and by the Puffin Shuttle walkers' bus. There are good shops, inns and guesthouses. There is ample parking at the head of the creek. Start this stretch from the village **32**, crossing the river from the car park and taking the footpath along the Gribin ridge **33**. Close to the seaward end of the ridge, descend to Gwadn **A**, cross the valley, and climb up to the Coast Path on the cliff top.

Dinas Fawr **34** is a lovely peninsula. There are some traces of an Iron Age fort, but most of the embankments and pits at the neck of the peninsula are the remains of an ancient copper mine worked in Tudor times. Enjoy the mass of wild flowers in the early summer. There are glorious views of the coast to east and west, and with luck you can watch gannets fishing in the bay.

The pebble beach at Newgale, formed by the storm waves that assault the coast of St Bride's Bay.

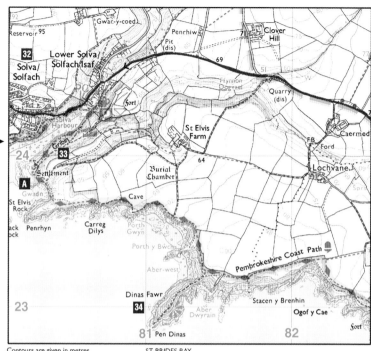

Reservoir 95
Gwar-y-coed
Penrhiw
Clover Hill
71
Pit (dis)
32
Lower Solva/
Solfach Isaf
69
Solva/
Solfach
Ffynnon
Dowrel
Quarry (dis)
Fort
51
Caermed
Silva
Harbour
St Elvis
Farm
FB
Ford
64
Lochvane
24
Gribin
33
Settlement
Burial
Chamber
A
Gwadn
Cave
St Elvis
Rock
Penrhyn
Carreg
Dilys
Porth
Gwyn
ack
ock
Porth y Bwch
Pembrokeshire Coast Path
Aber-west
Dinas Fawr
23
34
Stacen y Brenhin
Ogof y Cae
Aber
Dwyrain
Fort
81 Pen Dinas
82

Contours are given in metres
The vertical interval is 5m

ST BRIDES BAY

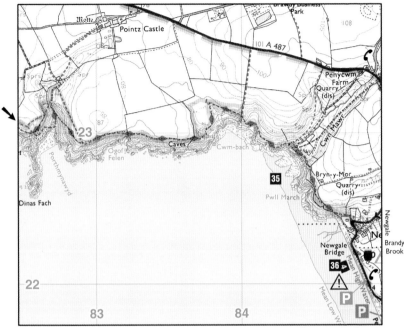

Contours are given in metres
The vertical interval is 5m

Dinas Fach, to the east, is a wild and jagged peninsula, with a spectacular blowhole close to its tip. In early summer, as you continue round the corner into Porthmynawyd, you are confronted by great sheets of blue vernal squill on the clifftop slope. This little valley is one of Pembrokeshire's surprises, with ferns, brambles, willow trees, sea buckthorn, flag irises and woodland birds. There is a small sandy beach, sometimes referred to as 'Pointz Castle Beach'.

Tucked into the north-eastern corner of St Bride's Bay, Penycwm beach **35** is easily accessible, with good footpaths from the hamlet on the main road. There are the remains of a small brickworks here, close to the cliff edge. The cottage was that of the manager. A tramway ran up the valley to the main road. A little way inland is the Brawdy military airfield (now closed). The site, now renamed Cawdor Barracks, is the HQ of the army's 14th Signals Division. At Whitehouse (about 2 miles inland) there is a popular youth hostel.

Spectacular exposures of Cambrian sedimentary rocks (sandstones, conglomerates, shales, fault breccias, etc.) can be examined here at low tide. If you follow the beach southwards be aware of the tide.

Newgale **36** is the most impressive sandy beach in Pembrokeshire, stretching for almost 2½ miles (4 km) towards Rickets Head. There is wonderful flat sand, and while Newgale is popular for bathing, you must watch out for a powerful undertow. The beach is becoming increasingly popular for surf-based sports. Brandy Brook marks

the western end of the Pembrokeshire Landsker – the invisible dividing line between the Welsh- and English-speaking parts of Pembrokeshire.

Follow the minor road, the pebble beach crest, or the sandy beach **B**. The going is easy on the beach, but be sure to rejoin the Coast Path near the beach café. The valley side and slopes above the northern car park give you your first sight of Pembrokeshire's Coal Measures. Note the traces of colliery waste, and the ubiquitous lime kilns. There were 26 shafts hereabouts in the 1800s. From the southern car park and beach café follow the road uphill and then return to the footpath proper when invited to do so by a fingerpost on your right.

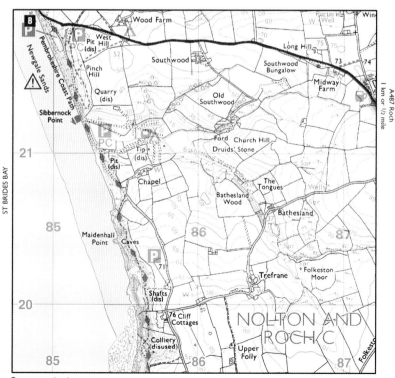

Contours are given in metres
The vertical interval is 5m

Trefane Cliff Colliery was worked from 1850 to 1905, with coal exported from Nolton Haven by sea and also from Haverfordwest. The coal was hauled initially in pairs of 8-ton trolleys by traction engines. You can see good traces of the colliery remains – the brick chimney stack, the foundations of the engine shed, the overgrown shaft, and piles of colliery waste and steam engine clinker. To the south you encounter many other traces of old coal workings. Rickets Head, with its characteristic profile projecting out into St Bride's Bay, should be renamed 'Rickety Head' since it is crumbling away, attacked on both sides by wave action.

Nolton Haven **37** (originally called 'Old Town') was one of the main coal-exporting points for the Nolton–Newgale Coalfield. Nolton village is located half a mile (1 km) from the beach, which has clean sands, popular bathing (but look out for currents at certain states of the tide), a good car park, and toilets. The inn is located close to the beach.

Madoc's Haven is an area of rapid erosion, so take extra care here. The beach escape path **C** that joins the Coast Path over a stile is a very steep and slippery descent. Druidston Haven **38** is named not after a druid but after Drue, one of the Norman knights who established himself in this area in the early 12th century.

You must now follow the track to the road, and then take the road uphill past Druidston Hotel before returning to the cliff top **D**. There is a path in front of the hotel and along the coast, but it is private. If you are still to be convinced about the effects of marine erosion, take a careful look at this stretch of coastline! The peninsula leading to Ladder Rock is not accessible from the National Trail; this is just as well, since it is very dangerous. Between Druidston Caves and Haroldston Chins you can see a range of quite spectacular cliff-collapse features – clifftop crevasses, rock falls, pinnacles, towers, stepped and faulted cliff faces, scree slopes and detached blocks. South of Haroldston Chins the vegetated cliff slope is littered with great blocks of rock.

On Black Point there is a simple Iron Age fort in a far from simple position. There are two hut circles on the peninsula. Look carefully at the landscape hereabouts, for it shows how rapidly certain processes can operate to change the appearance of the land surface. Modern landslides, which started in 1944 and and still continue, have transformed the landscape; in effect, the whole peninsula has dropped seawards. The landslide crevasses and escarpments can be seen adjacent to the

Nolton Haven, which was once an important coal exporting port.

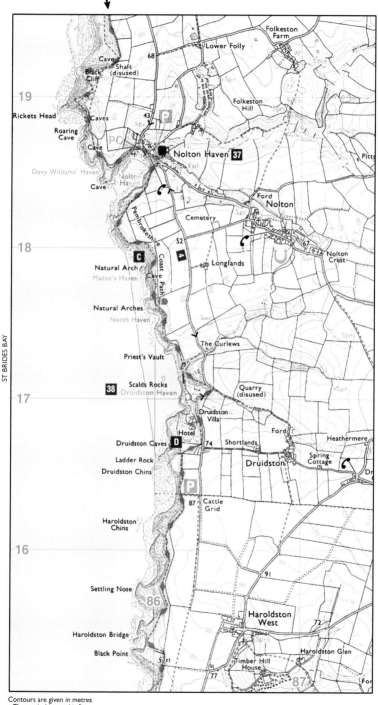

Contours are given in metres
The vertical interval is 5m

ST BRIDES BAY

footpath. About half a mile further south, the Sleek Stone is a textbook example of a monocline, easily seen from the footpath.

Broad Haven **39** has been a popular bathing beach since the early 1800s. A National Park information point is housed in the large and well-appointed youth hostel, located at the northern car park. Along the sea front to the south you will find a hotel, shop, post office and inn.

Look out for . . .

. . . the charming harbour of Solva **A**; the magnificent storm beach at Newgale **36** – a treasure trove for far-travelled glacial erratics; traces of the old coal industry at Trefran and Nolton.

Between Broad Haven and Little Haven the official Coast Path follows the road, which is narrow and can be dangerous during the peak summer season. If the tide is low, it is possible to walk on the beach around The Rain and past The Settlands to Little Haven, observing superb folding and faulting structures in the Coal Measure. You must, however, be sure of the state of the tide to avoid getting cut off in the Settlands.

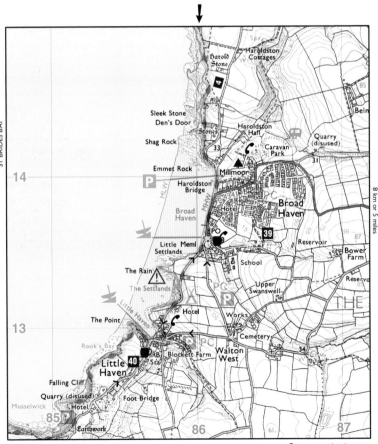

ST BRIDES BAY

B4341 Haverfordwest (Hwlffordd)
8 km or 5 miles

Contours are given in metres
The vertical interval is 5m

Railway Street in Saundersfoot. The railway line carried coal from the Stepaside and Kilgetty collieries to Saundersfoot Harbour.

The Pembrokeshire coal industry

The Pembrokeshire Coalfield is part of the South Wales Coalfield, isolated from the main coal-mining area and with the coal-bearing strata compressed and broken in such a way that exploitation has always been difficult. Nevertheless, Pembrokeshire was famous as the source of the world's finest anthracite, and it is said that Queen Victoria refused to allow coal from anywhere else to fire the boilers of her royal yachts.

Coal was being worked in crude open pits as far back as the 14th century, and traces of these old pits can still be found in the three main coal-mining districts – at the head of St Bride's Bay around Newgale, Nolton and Little Haven; around the inner part of the Milford Haven waterway; and in the Saundersfoot–Amroth area. By 1600, pits were being worked everywhere as the use of anthracite for domestic heating became more and more popular, and by 1700 demand was growing further afield. Soon coal was the main export from the Pembrokeshire ports, and for 200 years it

was the basis for most of the industrial activity of the county. By 1800 the coalfield had attained national importance and demand ran far ahead of supply. During the early 1800s annual production totals in excess of 150,000 tons were achieved regularly, but after 1865 production fell off gradually in the face of competition from the larger British coalfields. Also, the Pembrokeshire mines were never very well equipped, and underground conditions were appalling because of the narrow and fractured coal seams and because of drainage problems as shafts were driven deeper and deeper. Nevertheless, some of the collieries continued working until the last century, and the last mine, at Hook, was in use until 1948.

There are at least 140 abandoned mines in Pembrokeshire, and literally hundreds of abandoned bell-pits. Piles of colliery spoil can be seen from the Coast Path around Newgale, Nolton, Saundersfoot and Amroth; other relics of the industry include the stack of Trefrane Cliff Colliery near Newgale and Saundersfoot Harbour, which once looked down on a beach pitch black with coal dust.

7 Little Haven to Dale (via St Ann's Head)

19 ½ miles (31.4 km)
passing Musselwick and Marloes Sands

Ascent 2,477 feet (755 metres)
Highest point 262 feet (80 metres)

You can reach Little Haven **40** by a bus service from Haverfordwest and Broad Haven; the bus stop is at the top of the hill to the north of the village. There is also a seasonal walker's shuttle bus service. Starting this section of the walk in the centre of the village, follow the track out towards The Point and turn left on to the Coast Path.

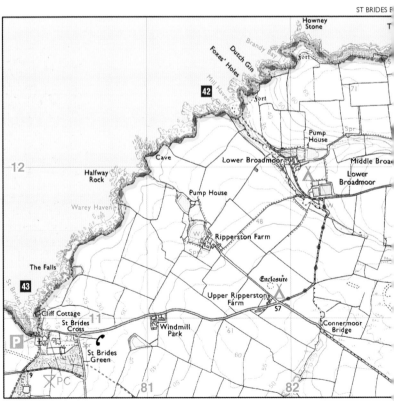

Contours are given in me
The vertical interval is

The gentle and well protected cliffs on the way to Borough Head come as a pleasant surprise, covered with glorious deciduous woodland. Below the Path is the site of an abandoned sailing lifeboat station which operated between 1882 and 1922. As you approach Borough Head **41**, look at the tree crowns. Salt spray and wind blasting have killed many of the topmost branches.

To the west of Borough Head **41** the coast is more exposed, and the path takes you eventually to the evocatively named inlets of Brandy Bay and Dutch Gin. Foxes' Hole is another inlet, this time cut along a great fault. Mill Haven **42** is a small, attractive cove accessible on foot from Lower Broadmoor Farm.

St Bride's Haven **43** is a pretty cove occupying the northern end of a broad valley that runs across the peninsula towards Dale. It offers bright red cliffs, a 'Victorianised' church, two walled gardens, and a large and well-built lime kiln. There is room to park up to 30 cars, and grassy banks for picnics. In the cliffs near the lime kiln, coastal retreat has exposed the ends of stone-lined coffins in the old graveyard. This is stately home territory. St Bride's Estate once belonged to the Barons of Kensington. Attractive parkland surrounds the Victorian 'castle' which was the baronial residence. The site has been redeveloped as a holiday complex.

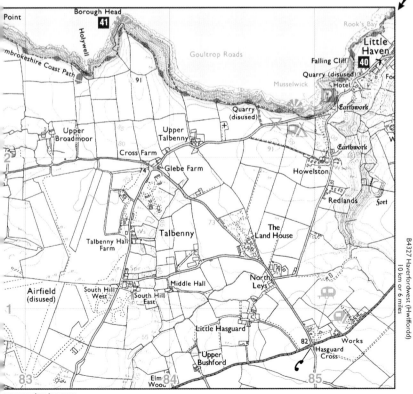

B4327 Haverfordwest (Hwlffordd)
10 km or 6 miles

tours are given in metres
e vertical interval is 5m

The National Trail follows the seaward boundary wall of the estate towards The Nab Head **44**, which is the site of Pembrokeshire's best-known Mesolithic flint-chipping floor. The name derives from the old word 'knap', meaning the process of striking flakes off flint nodules. To the south of Tower Point the Kensington Estate wall is particularly impressive. Note the buttresses and measures taken to continue the line of the wall across a deep gulley.

Musselwick Sands **45** is a lovely golden sandy beach, with reasonable access down a steep gulley. The beach is backed by high, dark-coloured, crumbly cliffs – do not get cut off by a rising tide, and do watch out for rock falls. There is good footpath access from the Marloes–Martin's Haven road.

Now the path takes you westwards along a fascinating stretch of coast with craggy rock outcrops on the cliff slopes. Soon you come to Martin's Haven **46**, the departure point for the Skomer Island boats and the 'port' for the village of Marloes. Very popular nowadays with the sub-aqua fraternity, it has a car park, toilets, information display about the Skomer Marine Reserve, and a sales point for the Wildlife Trust South and West Wales. There is severe congestion here at times in the main holiday season, both because of the narrow road access and because of the limited size of the car park. There is an inscribed Celtic ring-cross (more than 1,000 years old) in the Deer Park wall near the converted cottage.

Celtic ring-cross at Martin's Haven.

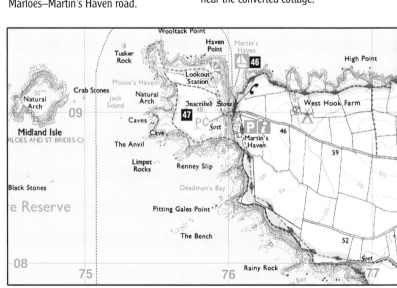

Contours are given in met
The vertical interval is 5r

The Deer Park **47** is contained by a stone wall built around 1800 as an embellishment to the St Bride's Estate. The wall runs parallel to an Iron Age embankment on the western side of a glacial meltwater channel. Explore the Deer Park if you have time. Out to the west you can see Midland Isle with Skomer beyond; and further away, to the

south-west, Skokholm (see page 132). Note also how the heathland in the centre of the peninsula gives way to coastal grassland, with thrift and prostrate broom on the exposed cliff edges.

From Renney Slip, follow the trail towards Rainy Rock and Albion Sands, passing a promontory fort with triple embankments

BRIDES BAY

Contours are given in metres
The vertical interval is 5m

Contours are given in metres
The vertical interval is 5m

and a good settlement platform. When you reach the promontory adjacent to Gateholm **A** you will encounter a footpath leading inland to the Marloes Sands Youth Hostel and car park. Here you can escape from the Coast Path if you do not wish to walk all the way to Dale.

The mainland promontory (Horse Neck) and Gateholm Island are made of Old Red Sandstone – the colour of the rocks is unmistakable. Beware of the tide if

Three Chimneys, Marloes Sands. Here alternating beds of Silurian sandstone and mudstone stand almost vertically.

you descend to the beach or cross to the island **48**. Gateholm and the adjacent coast have been occupied since Mesolithic times. The island once supported a sizeable population, and there are 130 hut-circles, indicating settlement in the Iron Age. Later, in the Age of the Saints, there may have been a Christian monastic community here.

Marloes Sands **49** is one of the most beautiful Pembrokeshire beaches. There is good bathing when the weather is calm. The most popular of three access routes is via a sunken lane and down the stream valley from the National Trust car park. At Three Chimneys, beds of alternating sandstone and mudstone stand almost vertically, with the 'chimneys' picked out by differential erosion.

The National Trail continues along the cliff tops, providing fine views of the beach below. As you approach Red Cliff you come upon the old RAF Dale aerodrome, later a Fleet Air Arm station, HMS *Goldcrest*, which closed in 1948. It is easy walking above Red Cliff and Hooper's Point. At The Hookses you may be surprised by the cottage nestling in its valley. There was also a farm here before the upper part of the valley was transformed by the building of the airfield.

Westdale Bay occupies the western end of an old river valley on the line of the Ritec fault, which extends east along the Milford Haven waterway from Dale. Bathing is dangerous; beware of a strong undertow on an ebbing tide. From here **B** you can either follow the path inland to Dale or continue southwards on the Trail. The full circuit of the peninsula will add about 5 miles (8 km) and 3 hours to your walk.

On the south shore of Westdale Bay, Great Castle Head supports a late Iron Age promontory fort. Inland near Long Point was the site of HMS *Harrier*, a Royal Navy radar and meteorological school. South of Short Point, a stile and gate in the National Trust embankment lead to the free Trust car park at Kete. This is a good start/finish point for those walking the full circuit of the Dale Peninsula.

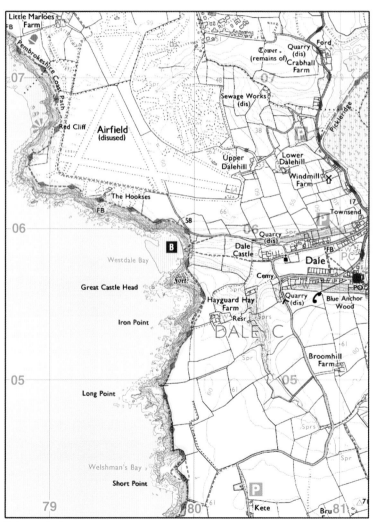

Contours are given in metres
The vertical interval is 5m

The western end of Marloes Sands, with the ancient settlement site of Gateholm in the distance.

Flowering sea thrift – ubiquitous around the whole of the Pembrokeshire coast during the early summer.

Above a little creek called The Vomit **50** the path joins the road from Dale. Here, on the southernmost tip of the Dale peninsula, there is no public access to the cliff tops, but there is a recently dedicated path to Cobbler's Hole, where there are dramatic folds in the rocks. St Ann's Head guards the approach to the Milford Haven waterway, and was the scene of one of the world's worst oil pollution disasters when the *Sea Empress* spilled 72,000 tonnes of crude oil into the sea in February 1996. On the western flank of the little peninsula is the former coastguard station, installed in 1966 in one of the two old lighthouses which closed in 1910. Until recently the converted building housed the Milford Haven Maritime Rescue Sub-Centre. The front light, lower down and closer to the tip of the headland, was built in 1841 as a replacement for an old coal-fired light tower. You may

walk south towards the lighthouse, but must then use the small gate in front of the round engine house and follow the marked path northwards across the field **C**. You will see an attractive row of old coastguard and Trinity House cottages. The walled garden and steps and the quay were built in 1800 for the import of building materials for the lighthouses and cottages.

Mill Bay **51** is where Henry Tudor landed with 2,000 men on 7 August 1485. From here he marched through Wales, and 15 days after his landing he and his allies won the famous battle for the English crown at Bosworth Field. From Mill Bay you follow the path eastwards. Close to three navigation towers (used by ships entering Milford Haven) there are gun emplacements associated with West Blockhouse. This open battery was in use during both world wars. West Blockhouse itself has been sensitively restored by the Landmark Trust for holiday letting.

Watwick Bay is a surprise, with clean golden sands, good bathing and a lush wooded valley. To the north-east, the Watwick Point light, about 160 feet (50 metres) high, is one of the essential navigational features maintained by the Port Authority for waterway shipping. Castlebeach Bay is at the mouth of another lush wooded valley, where you will find a ruined lime kiln. There is a small sandy beach, suitable for bathing.

Dale Fort **52** is Victorian, having been built as a component of the Haven defences between 1852 and 1856. Since 1947 the fort has belonged to the Field Studies Council. When you reach the road leading to the fort, turn left. As you walk you can look down into a dense deciduous woodland, well sheltered from the prevailing south-westerlies and far enough from the west coast to escape the worst effects of salt spray.

Dale **53** is an old trading and fishing port, one of the largest settlements of the Haven in Tudor times. Fishing, shipbuilding and general trading were the main activities, and the little port served a sizeable farming population. Now there are very few fishing boats in the village, and Dale has become a popular watersports centre. The beach is stony and rough, and there is a new car park to cater for the numerous summer visitors. There are toilets, shops, a café, public house, yacht club, landing stage and a windsurfing tuition centre.

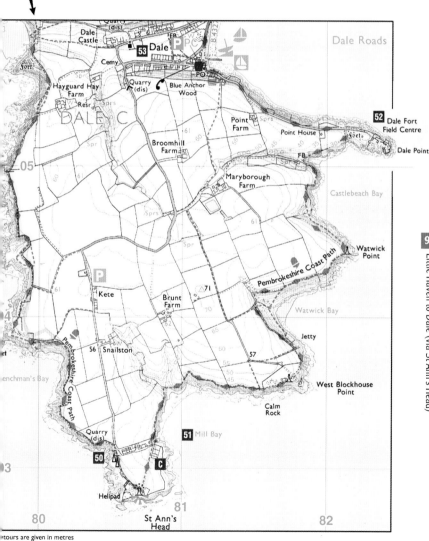

tours are given in metres
e vertical interval is 5m

8 Dale to Neyland

16 miles (25.7 km)
via Monk Haven and Milford Haven

Ascent 3,445 feet (1,050 metres)
Highest point 230 feet (70 metres)

Dale **53** is connected by a weekly bus service to and from Haverfordwest and by the Puffin Shuttle walkers' bus. The walk to Neyland takes you through oil refining country and also through an urban stretch through Milford Haven. You can follow a number of alternative routes through the built-up areas. There are a number of points at which care is needed if you are not to lose contact with the Coast Path – look out for waymarks on lampposts through Milford.

Start this stretch of the National Trail in Dale village, following the road northwards along the shore of the Gann Estuary. After about half a mile you will come to the Pickleridge car park **A**, passing two ruined lime kilns on your left. There are not many windmill remains left in Pembrokeshire, but behind you on the hillside is one of them. Probably it was used for corn milling.

On the west side of Pickleridge the lagoons are flooded gravel pits created in 1941–42 during the phase of wartime airfield construction. On the seaward side of the ridge are the extensive intertidal Gann Flats, widely used by marine biology students based at Dale Fort.

Before setting off from the Pickleridge car park to cover the stretch to Milford Haven, think very carefully about your timings. Consultation of the tide tables is essential. There are two places at which you have to cross tidal creeks – The Gann and Sandy Haven, both of which are submerged for most of the time. At The Gann you have six hours around low water in which to cross, and four hours at Sandy Haven. It will take you about two hours to walk between the two. So you should leave Pickleridge on a falling tide. If you get your timings wrong, you will have to walk three times as far to reach the eastern side of Sandy Haven, or else wade across Sandy Haven Creek.

The 'high-water detour' at The Gann is as follows. Take the road northwards to

Look out for . . .

. . . the tidal flats between Pickleridge and Mullock Bridge, periodically inundated by high tides; the colourful tidal creek of Sandy Haven **55**; the Victorian defences at South Hook Fort, Stack Rock and Fort Hubberston; the installations of the oil and LNG industries; the old fishing port and modern marina at Milford Haven **57**.

Mullock Bridge; cross the bridge and take the Milford Haven fork **B**; opposite Mullock Farm entrance turn right and follow the path as far as Slatehill Farm. Turn right at the farm and then left, following the field boundary. Then turn either right or left to reach the coast. The route along the shore of the estuary can be used except during stormy high tides. If you follow the shore, look out for the fingerpost showing where the Coast Path leaves the beach.

Monk Haven **54** is a surprise and a joy. The lovely wooded valley runs up towards the village of St Ishmael's. The massive castellated wall that runs across the valley at high-tide level was built as part of the Trewarren Estate, probably in the 1700s. On the east side of the creek the watchtower near the point is a Victorian folly. Around Watch House Point there is an assortment of lookout and artillery positions dating from the First World War, both above and below the trail.

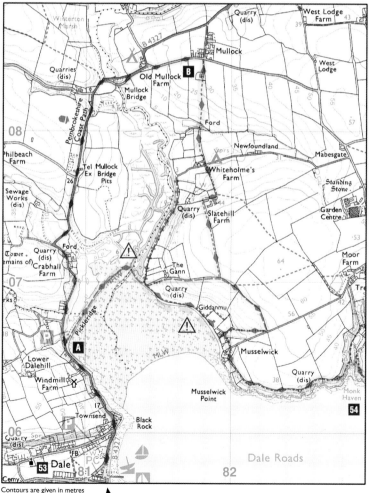

Contours are given in metres
The vertical interval is 5m

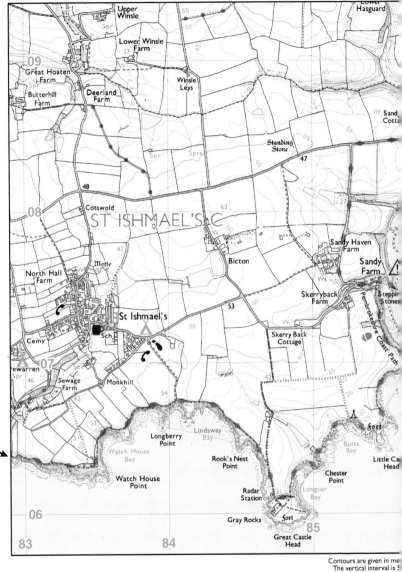

Contours are given in me
The vertical interval is 5

Lindsway Bay, accessible via a steep path and easily reached by the footpath from St Ishmael's, is chiefly notable as the place where HRH The Prince of Wales first set foot on Welsh soil in 1955.

As you follow the trail south-eastwards, you come to Great Castle Head, which has an extensive Iron Age fort defended by a single embankment and ditch. The scanning radar visible out on the headland is part of the waterway navigational system.

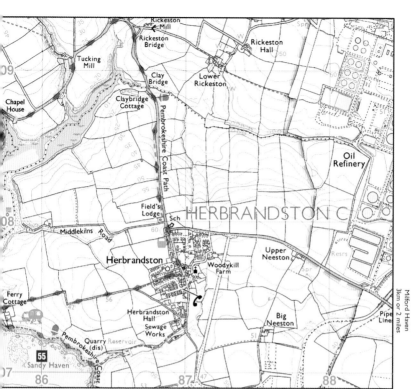

Contours are given in metres
The vertical interval is 5m

Sandy Haven **55** can be reached by road via Sandy Haven Farm, or via the village of Herbrandston. There are a few cottages here, on the western side of the creek near the old ferry landing. This is a lovely spot, with Sandyhaven Pill emptied and filled with every tidal cycle. If your timing is right (you have four hours), you can now cross on the stepping stones without getting your feet wet; if not, you have a very long detour inland around the Pill.

The high-water detour is as follows. Take the road northwards past Sandy Haven Farm. Turn right on reaching the Dale–Milford road, and follow this road via Rickeston Bridge and Clay Bridge, and then on the permissive path to

Herbrandston. At the church hall turn right to follow the footpath and then the lane down to the Pill. Follow the shore southwards, skirting the caravan park and walking along the clifftop footpath.

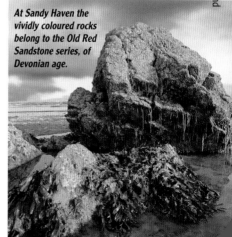

At Sandy Haven the vividly coloured rocks belong to the Old Red Sandstone series, of Devonian age.

South of Sandy Haven beach you cannot escape the influence of the Milford Haven oil and gas industry **56**. The jetty is now used for liquified natural gas (LNG). Adjacent to the path you will see a series of old gun emplacements from the First World War. Offshore you can see Stack Rock Fort, one of the Victorian defences of the waterway. In its heyday (1870) it supported an armament of 23 turret guns and a garrison of 168 men. South Hook Fort, located on the landward side of the Coast Path, was completed in 1863, and was designed so that its batteries could complement those of Stack Rock Fort. The defensible barracks, whose massive bulk can be glimpsed over the 'cosmetic' embankment built by Esso, had a garrison of 180 men.

As you pass under the landward end of the refurbished LNG jetty, you leave the National Park. Follow the road past the housing estate and continue downhill past the Murco jetty access point.

Gelliswick Bay is the headquarters of the Pembrokeshire Yacht Club, and the local beach for the communities of Hubberston and Hakin. It is dominated to the west by the Murco jetty and to the east by Fort Hubberston. This particular fort, completed in 1865, had a garrison of 250 men, and the gun emplacements (as at South Hook Fort) supported 28 guns.

Halfway up the hill **C**, turn right up the steps, follow the track adjacent to the school playing field, turn right at the school, and then follow the most obvious route to the Victoria Bridge at the head of Milford Docks. This means following Picton Road, Spike's Lane and St Anne's Road.

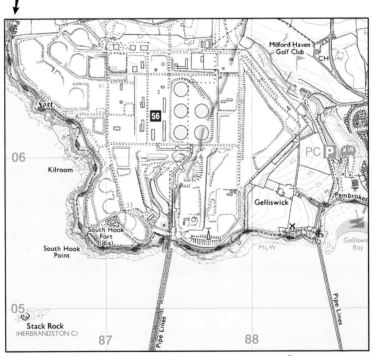

Contours are given in metres
The vertical interval is 5m

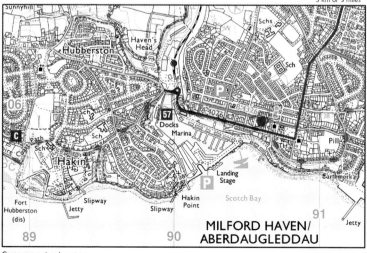

Milford Docks **57** have had a chequered history. The new town of Milford was planned in 1790, with the docks as the focus. Originally it was intended to establish a naval dockyard here and to develop the Irish packet trade, but at the time money was in short supply and both the Admiralty and the Irish Mail moved to Pembroke Dock. The docks were not completed until 1888. Hopes of attracting transatlantic passenger traffic never materialised, but gradually the town's fishing industry expanded and between 1900 and 1914 Milford joined the top league of fishing ports. Now there are only a few trawlers based here, and the docks have been transformed by activity centred on the Milford Marina, with many new commercial and leisure developments.

Follow Hamilton Terrace along the lower edge of the town. The street is named after Sir William Hamilton, the town's founder, who died in 1803. Turn right along the Rath and pass the Rock Gardens and old swimming pool. Follow Murray Road and then turn right down Cellar Hill. Take the path halfway down and you will eventually gain access to the western shore of Castle Pill. On the

A4076(T) Johnston
5 km or 3 miles

MILFORD HAVEN/
ABERDAUGLEDDAU

Contours are given in metres
The vertical interval is 5m

Isambard Kingdom Brunel, who was influential in bringing the Great Western Railway to the old rail terminus at Neyland.

western side of the Pill entrance there used to be a shipbreaking yard, while to the east are the substantial buildings of the old Royal Naval Armaments Depot, closed in 1991. Follow the shore or footpath northwards, then take the road to the causeway which crosses the Pill.

Having crossed Black Bridge, follow the B4325 up the hill and towards Waterston. This is a dangerous stretch – there is no pavement and traffic travels fast. If you want to play it safe, walk uphill through the housing estate. Near Hill Crest cottage, turn right **D** and follow the lane southwards to Venn Farm, then follow the fingerposts. The National Trail is easy to follow along the southern edge of the LNG tank farm (2 miles/ 3.2 km). The extraordinary steel tunnel and cages, which take you across the pipelines connecting jetties and storage tanks, are yet another of the

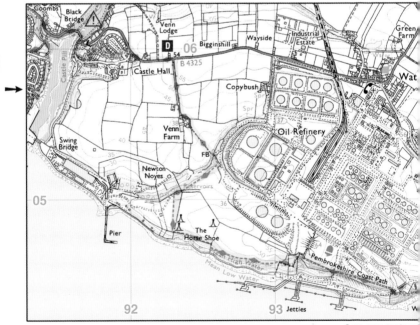

Contours are given in met
The vertical interval is 5

footpath's eccentric surprises. You continue to the metal cage over the jetty approach road, and the Coast Path drops down to sea level to the east of Wear Point. You then continue with a pleasant, easy walk towards Hazelbeach. There are several well-maintained seats and fine views across the waterway towards Pembroke Dock, and upstream towards Cleddau Bridge.

At Hazelbeach, close to The Ferry Inn, you will find toilets, car parking spaces, and access to the shore. Now you continue eastwards on the road, passing Llanstadwell Church with its typical castellated 'Little England' tower. Church and churchyard are beautifully situated right on the edge of the waterway. Turn right on to the main road (B4325), then go past the Neyland Yacht Club and the Brunel Hotel, and down to Brunel Quay. Here there is a large car park.

Neyland **58**, like Milford, is a planned town, but about 50 years younger. It owes its origin to Isambard Kingdom Brunel, who made it the terminus for his South Wales Railway in 1856. For almost half a century the town thrived, with a fishing industry, ice factory, shipyard, and busy sea traffic for the Irish packet service. Lord Beeching's famous axe fell upon the railway in 1965, and eight years later the ferry service disappeared as well. Now, after a period of decline, Neyland is picking up again. Brunel Quay, once busy with rail sidings and quayside activity, has seen a carefully planned resurgence. The marina was the catalyst, and now there is a terminus for pleasure cruises on the waterway, a chandlery, cafeteria and shop, new factory units and new housing developments.

A477 Haverfordwest (Hwlffordd)
11km or 7 miles

A44 Pembroke
5 km or 3 miles

The Milford Haven oil and gas industry

The oil industry came to Milford Haven in the late 1950s as the oil companies began to plan for the use of supertankers to transport Middle Eastern crude oil to Britain. These tankers were being designed to carry ever-larger tonnages, and deep-water berthing facilities were required that could handle vessels of 300,000 tons or more. Milford Haven appeared ideal for development. In 1957–58, work began on the creation of a major oil port right on the edge of the National Park.

The first refinery built was the Esso refinery at Herbrandston, which came on-stream in 1960. The BP Ocean Terminal, on the south shore near the old Popton Point fort, was opened in 1961. Some land at Kilpaison in Angle Bay was used for a crude-oil tank-farm, but BP did not build a refinery here; instead they

Milford marina and docks.

constructed a 62-mile (100-km) pipeline to their Llandarcy refinery (now closed), capable of pumping 10 million tons of crude oil per year. Next came the Texaco refinery near Pembroke. This was the company's only UK refinery, and today (under the ownership of Chevron) it has a refining capacity of 10.5 million tonnes per year. In 1968 the Gulf Oil refinery was opened near Waterston, with a three-berth jetty quite close to the shore. This was the only Milford Haven refinery with an associated petrochemical plant. Finally, in 1973, the Amoco refinery (now owned by Murco) came on-stream, the only one located away from the coast. It is served by a long jetty quite close to the South Hook jetty and adjacent to Gelliswick Bay.

The oil industry has brought with it a variety of ancillary developments. The most prominent was the Pembroke power

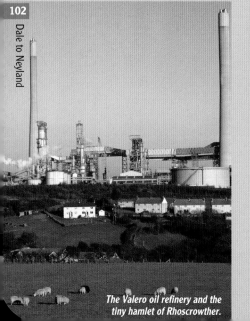

The Valero oil refinery and the tiny hamlet of Rhoscrowther.

station, completed in 1975 and intended to burn heavy fuel oil for the generation of 2,000 megawatts for the grid. The huge chimney stack, 750 feet (230 metres) high, was visible from all over West Wales; and the double row of 400-kilovolt supergrid power lines makes a dramatic and not very beautiful impact on the Pembrokeshire landscape. Inland, the reservoir at Llysyfran was built to provide water for the oil industry. A pipeline was constructed to carry refined products to conveniently placed distribution centres in England, and the Port Authority undertook a programme of rock dredging in the deep-water channel, together with the installation of transit lights and other navigational aids, some of which the walker passes on the Coast Path.

The Esso refinery closed in 1983 and the BP Ocean Terminal shortly afterwards. The latest phase in Milford Haven's development involves the importation and regasification of LNG from the Middle East. The two major developments are at South Hook (on the old Esso refinery site) and Dragon LNG (on the old Gulf refinery site). Refurbishment projects have also been undertaken at the two remaining refineries to meet the demands for cleaner fuels and reduced pollution. Pembroke power station eventually became something of a 'white elephant'; in 1996 it stopped generating, and was then demolished. A new 2,000 megawatt power station, fuelled by LNG, is now operating.

Two events brought the local oil industry to world attention in 1996 – the *Sea Empress* disaster at the mouth of the waterway, and the proposal (defeated by massive public protest) to burn the highly controversial fuel orimulsion in the power station.

9 Neyland to Angle

17 miles (22.5 km)
through Pembroke Dock and Pembroke

Ascent 2,362 feet (720 metres)
Highest point 197 feet (60 metres)

Neyland **58** is a convenient stopping/ starting point, with good bus links from Haverfordwest, Milford Haven and Pembroke Dock. The town centre is within easy walking distance of Brunel Quay **59**, where refreshments are available. To continue on the Coast Path start at the Brunel Quay car park. Walk up the hill and turn right into Cambrian Road. When the road swings left, take the path to the right. Follow the path through the woods until you reach the A477 road. Turn right, cross the bridge and continue to the Cleddau Bridge proper. There is car parking space at the junction with the road to Burton Ferry.

The Cleddau Bridge was built between 1967 and 1975 in order to improve communications between the two shores of the waterway. As you cross the bridge, note the contrast between the views upstream and downstream.

You now embark upon a 'town trail' through Pembroke Dock. At the new roundabout near the southern end of the bridge, turn right past the Cleddau Hotel and follow Essex Road downhill to meet the A477 road near the large roundabout. Cross the road and follow Western Way, then turn right into Front Street. At the western end of the street is the massive defensive wall of the Royal Naval Dockyard **60** and the Martello tower, built around 1850, which was a part of the dockyard defensive system. It is now a little museum.

Turn left at The Shipwright's Arms and walk straight up Commercial Row, ffollowing the Pembroke signs. Leave the road and follow the path up to the Defensible Barracks, the most impressive local reminder of the dockyard's Victorian military defences. Turn left and follow the roadway towards Bethany Baptist Church, where you turn right and go downhill. At the dip in the road **B**, follow the tarmac path off to your left, along the edge of a little valley. Continue down Sycamore Street, cross the stile, and follow the footpath proper, with your route pointed out again by a fingerpost. Be sure to turn left off the track where indicated; follow the fingerposts and do not continue towards the sea. For half a mile or so the path runs across farmland before entering woodland near Bush School. The limestone quarries in the woods were used to provide the stone for Pembroke Castle and the walls and other buildings of the medieval town.

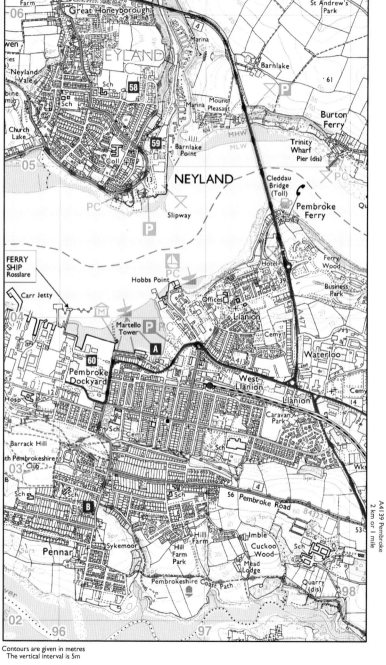

Contours are given in metres
The vertical interval is 5m

The immense Norman fortress of Pembroke Castle, built between 1190 and 1245 by William Marshal and his sor

Where the National Trail joins the road, turn right to the Castle Pond. At the pond either turn left into the town (the path is flooded on spring high tides) or right over the dam towards Monkton. Pembroke Castle **61** dominates the scene, and is one of the most powerful of the Norman fortresses in Wales. The present castle was built for the most part in the period 1190–1245 by William Marshal and his sons. Its most impressive feature is the Great Keep (the finest of its kind in Britain), which provides a commanding view in all directions. During the Middle Ages the castle was the key to the control of Little England, strategically located right in the heartland of the Anglo-Norman colony. It never fell to the Welsh. In 1457 Henry Tudor was born in the castle. The old walled town of Pembroke

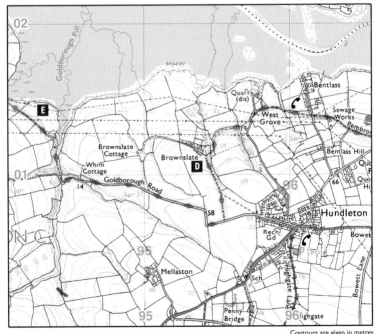

Contours are given in metres
The vertical interval is 5m

62 was created by the Normans; traces of the walls can still be seen, especially around St Michael's Tower and on the south side of the town.

Follow the path which runs round the castle and continue to Monkton. There are some fascinating buildings here – the Old Hall, the remains of the Old Priory, and the fine spacious church. Turn right and take the pedestrianised lane past the Old Hall. The National Trail then follows the B4320 road westwards.

After half a mile or so you leave the main road (do not continue round the corner) and drop down into the valley between the new bungalows **C**. Go past Quoits Mill Dam and continue to follow the lane uphill. Turn right when you encounter the fingerpost.

Now, having bid farewell to the medieval splendours of Pembroke and Monkton,

you return to the modern world! This is an electrical landscape; everything is dwarfed by the 180-foot (55-metre) pylons that connect Pembroke power station to the supergrid.

When you reach Brownslate you must follow the farm lane southwards **D**, although your instinct tells you that you should continue to head west. Turn right when you reach the road, and follow the road westwards for about half a mile (1 km). On rounding the corner after Whim Cottage, strike off the road and cross the stile on your right. Follow the little valley towards the head of Goldborough Pill. Soon you will pass a huge square lime kiln with hinges which held iron doors across the entrance. Now, after swinging west again, you climb a steep lane through the wood to pass, dwarfed, beneath the electricity cables **E**.

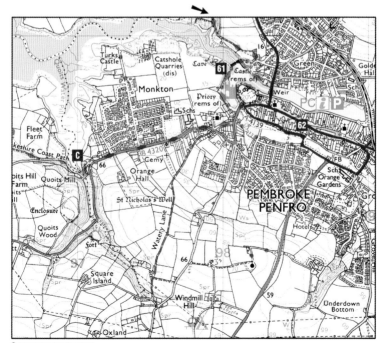

Contours are given in metres
The vertical interval is 5m

The Path climbs through Lambeeth Farm, and soon you can enjoy good views in all directions. To the east, Pembroke River estuary is a fine area for waders and other waterfowl, especially during the winter.

Follow the Path south of the power station approach road **63** and then cross the road **F** and follow the Path till you reach a gate. Turn left and then right, following the road past Pwllcrochan Church.

Martin's Haven inlet provides access on to Pwllcrochan Flats, once famous for their oyster and cockle fishery. If you feel like a short detour you can walk down to the shore on the western side of the creek, leaving the road adjacent to the bridge. Near the bridge, wild celery and marshmallow grow on the saltmarsh.

Continue along the lane, heading north-west. From the field at the end you have an excellent view of the Chevron refinery **64**, which is now, following various expansion and conversion projects, the largest refinery on the Haven. After traversing several fields, the Path descends and then runs under the base of the jetty. It has five berths, the largest of which can handle 300,000-ton supertankers.

The Path continues via Bullwell Bay. As you climb out of the bay you pass the

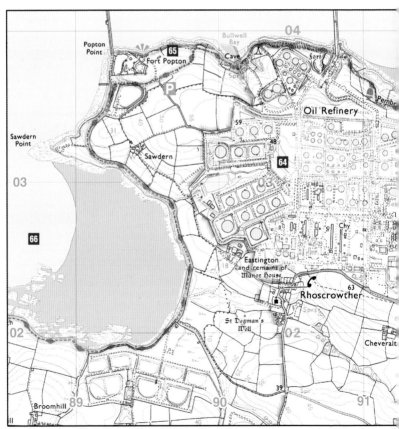

Contours are given in me
The vertical interval is 5

jetty once used for the import of crude oil to the BP Ocean Terminal. Soon you approach Fort Popton **65**, another of the Victorian defences, built around 1860. After the closure of the BP Ocean Terminal the building was converted for office and laboratory use, and for some years it housed a Field Studies Council Research Centre specialising in oil pollution studies.

Continue past the old oil tank site and descend towards the shore of Angle Bay **66**. Walking is easy on the asphalt service road built by BP. There is a car park near the old pumping station. The route now follows the low cliff. It is a gentle walk, along level ground without any stiles, but it can be rough going depending on field cultivation and season.

Tightly folded sedimentary rocks, Pwllcrochan – best seen at low tide.

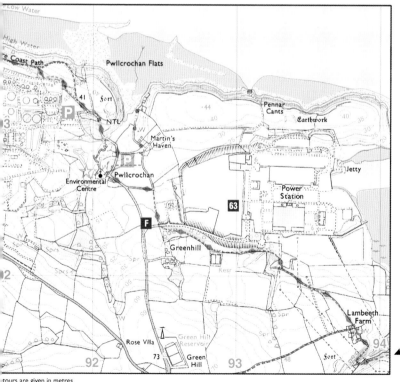

tours are given in metres
e vertical interval is 5m

Angle Bay **66** and its extensive mudflats are important winter feeding grounds for birds. There are many different habitats: calcareous mudflats, saltings, bare intertidal rocky areas, gravel beds and coarse pebble beaches. Eventually, near the Lodge, you enter the grounds of the Hall and walk above the wall towards Angle.

The little creek **67** is charming, with a ruined quay, old harbour walls, and a long gravel ridge projecting out from the northern shore. There are always a few small boats here, and there are traces of two rotting hulks. The footbridge **G** marked on the map no longer exists; you are *not* advised to try to take a shortcut to the public house on the way

to Angle Point! Continue to the village on the southern side of the creek.

Angle **68** is a single-street village flanked by remnants of the medieval strip-field system. The map shows how the main hedge boundaries run up-slope, at right angles to the main road. There are a number of interesting buildings, including the Georgian-style Globe Hotel, a fortified tower house, a medieval dovecote, and the remains of a supposed nunnery on the south side of the road. At the back of the church is a little Fisherman's Chapel above a vaulted crypt, built in 1447. The village has a shop, accommodation and public houses.

> **Look out for . . .**
> . . . the old railway terminal and quays at Neyland **58**; the old Royal Naval Dockyard at Pembroke Dock **60**; the immense Norman fortress of Pembroke Castle **61**; Victorian fortifications at Fort Popton and Chapel Bay; the mudflats **66** of Angle Bay, perfect territory for many wading birds.

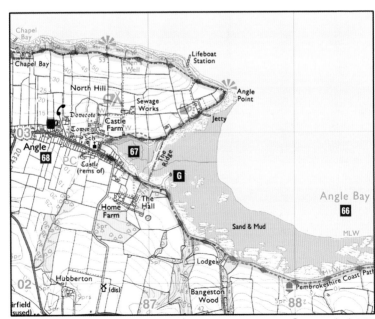

Contours are given in metres
The vertical interval is 5m

Short Sunderland flying boat at Pembroke Dock in 1931. The waterway was an important base for these aircraft during the Second World War.

The Royal Naval Dockyard

Begun in 1814, the Royal Naval Dockyard at Pembroke Dock was once the world's finest, most innovative shipbuilding yard. It was located here partly because of the sheltered deep-water anchorage, partly because of its remoteness from France, and partly because of a long tradition of local shipbuilding.

It grew rapidly, and because it was a strategically safe base for technological experiments, vessels were soon being built with steam propulsion, with paddles and with screw propellers, and with iron cladding. Warships were also increasing rapidly in size. The year 1834 saw the launching of the *Tartarus*, the Navy's first steam man-of-war. The *Conflict* of 1846 was the first warship fitted with a screw propeller. In 1847 the yard launched the *Lion*, the Navy's largest warship. In 1852 the *Duke of Wellington* was launched, being the largest three-decker in the world.

Five royal yachts were built here, and year after year naval barques, brigantines, cruisers, gunboats and battleships were completed for the fleet. In all, the dockyard saw the construction of more than 250 naval vessels, with a peak output of 23 ships in a single year. In the later years of the 19th century, at the peak of its fame, the dockyard employed over 3,000 men. Around the turn of the century the dockyard specialised in cruisers and battleships, and submarines were also built here during the First World War. But after the war, shipbuilding activity declined sharply so the Navy abruptly closed the yard in 1925, heralding an era of severe local hardship.

During the Second World War the dockyard saw a new lease of life, with some ship-repairing work and the co-ordination of mine-laying, mine-sweeping and Atlantic convoy escort work. Pembroke Dock had a major Sunderland flying boat base (celebrated in a new Flying Boat Exhibition Centre), and important fuel storage depots were established at both Llanion and Llanreath. However, the military installations inevitably attracted enemy attention, and the town suffered heavily from air raids, particularly in 1940–41.

Since the war the dockyard has had a chequered history, but much of it is still in use and the western part was until recently in the possession of the Admiralty. The great defensive walls of the dockyard are more or less intact; the Martello towers still stand sentinel where the dockyard walls reach the sea; and many of the dock basins and solid Victorian dockyard buildings can be seen very close to the recommended route through the town.

Neyland to Angle

10 Angle to Bosherston

17 ¾ miles (28.6 km)
negotiating the Castlemartin firing ranges

Ascent 2,116 feet (645 metres)
Highest point 230 feet (70 metres)

There is no regular bus service to Angle, but the Coastal Cruiser walkers' bus links the village with Pembroke and Pembroke Dock. The Havenlink water bus also calls here. There is limited car parking in the village **68**. The first part of this walk follows the coast, with varied cliff scenery. The second part involves a long inland detour on the periphery of the Ministry of Defence firing range. Try to arrange this walk for a weekend; this will at least allow you to visit part of the limestone coast of the Castlemartin peninsula.

You start this stretch on the North Hill circuit by walking eastwards towards Angle Point. The Old Point House Inn (supposedly 16th-century) is one of the few inns on the National Trail, and very atmospheric. The pub fire is reputed never to have gone out during the last 300 years. Just off the path is the old lifeboat station, clearly recognisable in spite of its ruinous condition. The modern lifeboat station, opposite the South Hook LNG terminal, is the only one on the Haven, well sheltered from the south-westerlies.

Continuing eastwards, you pass close to

Look out for . . .
. . . West Angle Bay **69**, where the ecology has made an amazing recovery since the *Sea Empress* disaster; the sand dune expanses of Broomhill and Brownslade; the Green Bridge of Wales; St Govan's Chapel.

the Chapel Bay cottages and then, following the track, on the landward side of Chapel Bay Fort, which is now being renovated. Soon Thorn Island comes into view. The island fort, built in 1954, is still in a good state of repair. It has had a chequered history, with a succession of owners seeking to run it as a somewhat quirky hotel for those who *really* want to get away from it all.

West Angle Bay **69** is a classic geological site. Look at the complicated geological structures and changes of rock type in the little coves on the north side of the bay. At the head of the beach there is a car park, telephone, toilets, caravan park and café. Behind the café are the remains of the brickworks; clay was excavated from a pit beside the toilet block.

Going west, you reach a disused RAF radio station, with old buildings. The modern building, formerly an RAF radar station, has been used for university radar research into offshore wave characteristics. Nearby, in a sweep overlooking the coast, are the gun emplacements of East Block House **70**, built around 1854. The old building that teeters on the edge of the cliff is the Elizabethan East Block House, built soon after the Spanish Armada sent a shiver down the spine of Britain.

The path runs past the Victorian battery and the remains of East Block House **A**. On the mainland adjacent to Sheep Island you come across an Iron Age defended site, and a lookout post dating from 1914–18. Across a rather dangerous isthmus there is an extensive area with hut circles and platforms, but it is not for the faint-hearted. There are further settlement traces on Sheep Island. As on Gateholm, the huts seem to have been built during the Age of the Saints. As you walk south-eastwards you see traces inland of Angle airfield **71**, built in the winter of 1940–41.

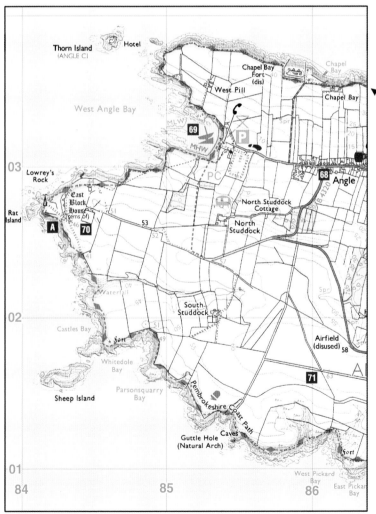

Contours are given in metres
The vertical interval is 5m

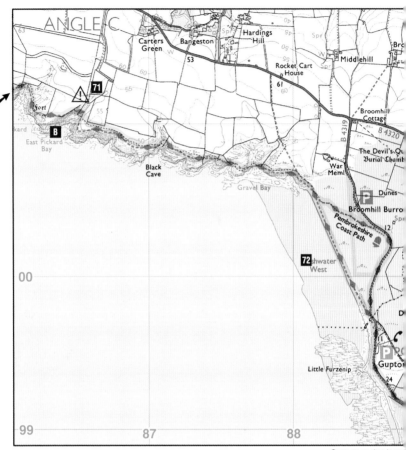

Contours are given in metres
The vertical interval is 5

Pick your way along the west side of East Pickard Bay following the marked route **B**, among the great jumble of Old Red Sandstone outcrops and fallen blocks. From either side of the bay there are views of the huge embankment built along the southern edge of the old Angle airfield **71**. The path is steep and slippery in places; be very careful in wet weather.

After $\frac{1}{2}$ mile or so, you reach Freshwater West **72**, one of the most spectacular bays in Pembrokeshire, with a superb sweep of sands extending for about 2 $\frac{1}{2}$ miles (4 km). It is served by the Coastal Cruiser

bus, but there can be summer congestion since car parking is limited. The beach looks inviting, but beware of a dangerous undertow on the ebb tide, and also of quicksands near the north end of the beach around low-water mark. The bay is famous for its sand dunes, or burrows.

This was once a great area for the collection of 'laver bread' from the intertidal rock outcrops. The thatched seaweed-storage hut on the grassy bank above Little Furzenip is the last one in Pembrokeshire, rebuilt by the National Park Authority in 2000.

From Little Furzenip the intertidal area round Great Furzenip and on Frainslake Sands is within the Ministry of Defence firing ranges and out of bounds. Phone 01646 662367 for range closed times. Near Gupton Farm, you should follow the Castlemartin Range Trail (partly off road) into Castlemartin. Castlemartin village has a substantial castle mound and a magnificent cattle pound. There was a pound here in 1480, but the present one dates from 1780 and was restored in 1972.

CASTLEMARTIN RANGE WARNING

All visitors to Castlemartin Range must note that this is a Ministry of Defence Range and the public have no right of access when firing is taking place.

General instructions

1. Keep within waymarks on each path. Do not leave these marked paths.
2. Comply with the public notices at all times.
3. Do not touch or pick up any ammunition or any other object you may see.
4. Please do not enter any buildings.
5. Please protect the wildlife. Do not take specimens.
6. Camping or making fires is not permitted.

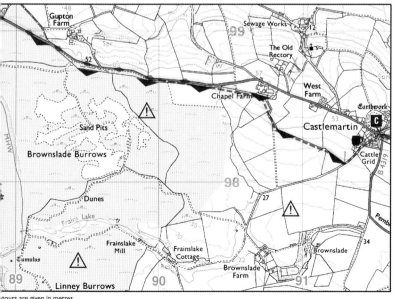

tours are given in metres
e vertical interval is 5m

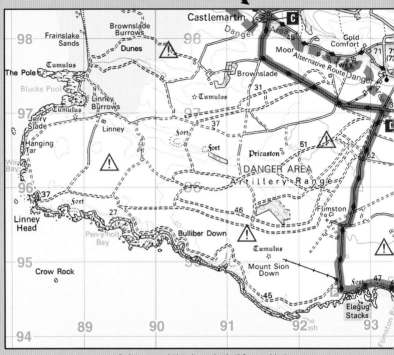

Scale is approx 1 1/8 inches to 1 mile (1.8 cm to 1 km)

It is always advisable to check the range firing schedules before proceeding beyond Castlemartin; see the local press for details of firing times or ask for advice at any tourist information centre.

The path from grid ref. 915 978 through Brownslade Farm and on around the coast to grid ref. 926 946 (see detailed map on page 133) is out of bounds to the public. However, during the year there are a number of guided walks organised by the National Park Authority within the range. Contact any tourist information centre for more details, or check on the web.

From Castlemartin, if the B4319 south is closed at gate C due to range activity, you can follow an off-road alternative trail towards gate D. This route also provides views across the range; you can watch the tank manoeuvres and firing practice. At **D**, you can then follow the road eastwards, passing Merrion Camp on your right. To your left you will see the tall steeple of Warren Church. This was derelict for many years but a daunting restoration project was completed and the church opened again for worship in 1988. Merrion Camp was established to provide training facilities and firing ranges for troops of the Royal Armoured Corps. The range is owned by MOD and is used by troops from many NATO countries.

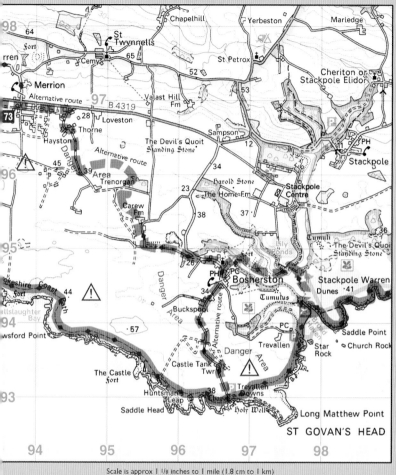

Scale is approx 1 1/8 inches to 1 mile (1.8 cm to 1 km)

When you have passed Merrion Camp, turn right off the road and follow the permissive bridleway which will take you past Thorne and eventually to join the Bosherston road near Carew Farm. You can then continue to Bosherston, where further options present themselves.

If you arrive at Gate D and find that it is open, follow the road southwards towards Flimston, the Green Bridge of Wales and Stack Rocks. Flimston Chapel is worth visiting en route to the coast, and it is open during the summer months. In the churchyard some large glacial erratics have been used as grave headstones. There is good car parking at Stack Rocks.

There is pleasant clifftop walking as you turn eastwards to follow the south shore of the Castlemartin peninsula. Be careful not to walk too close to the unstable cliff edge.

Broomhill Burrows, an area of dunes at Freshwater West formed from sand grains blown inland from the beach.

Probably the most photographed coastal feature in Pembrokeshire, the Green Bridge of Wales **74** is a textbook example of a natural arch, sweeping across a void and about 80 feet (24 metres) above the level of the sea. There is a good viewing platform near the range boundary fence; from the same point you can see two other arches.

A little way to the east, Stack Rocks (locally known as Elegug Stacks after the Welsh name for the guillemot) are also easily viewed from the cliff top. These tall pinnacles of rock, the remnants of past arches, provide safe nesting sites for the largest seabird colonies to be seen anywhere along the Coast Path.

If the 'Range East' section of the National Trail is open, you may now continue eastwards on a well-marked bridleway. First you encounter Flimston Castles, basically a peninsula made of near-vertical beds of limestone, but riddled with caves. Across the neck of the peninsula there are two embankments and ditches, indicating

The Green Bridge of Wales, a magnificent natural arch on the limestone coast of the Castlemartin peninsula.

Angle to Bosherston

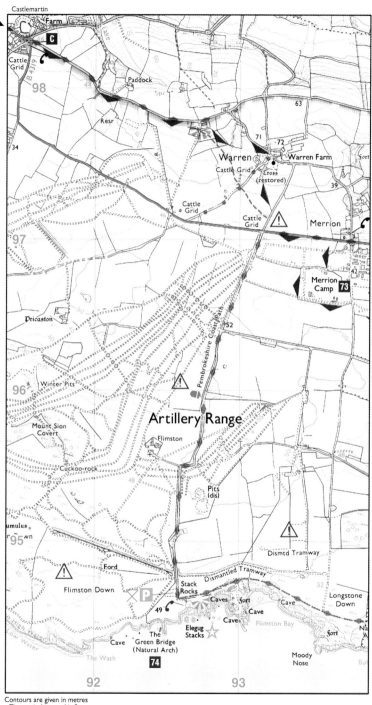

Contours are given in metres
The vertical interval is 5m

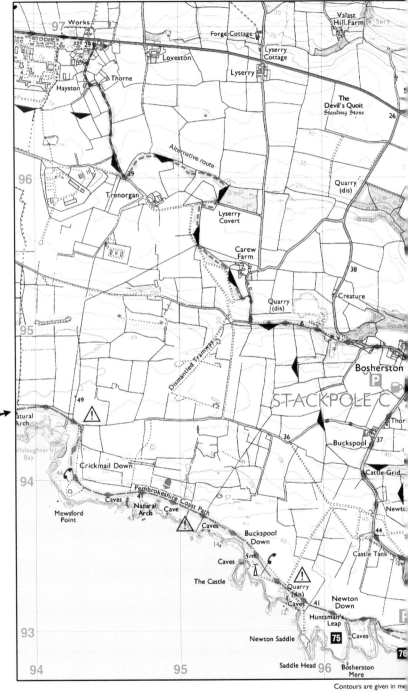

Angle to Bosherton

Works
97
Forge Cottage
Lyserry Cottage
Loveston
Lyserry
29
Thorne
Hayston
The Devil's Quoit
Standing Stone
26

Alternative route
96
39
Quarry (dis)
Trenorgan
Lyserry Covert
Carew Farm
38
Creature
Quarry (dis)
95
Dismantled Tramway
Quarry (dis)
Bosherston
P
49
STACKPOLE C
Natural Arch
36
Thor
Buckspool
37
llslaughter Bay
Crickmail Down
Cattle Grid
94
46
Pembrokeshire Coast Path
Caves
41
Natural Arch
Cave
57
Mewsford Point
Cave
Caves
Buckspool Down
40
Caves
fort
9
14
Castle Tank
Caves
44
The Castle
Quarry (dis)
Caves
Newton Down
41
Newt
45
93
12
Huntsman's Leap
Caves
75
Newton Saddle
76
94
95
Saddle Head
96
Bosherston Mere

Contours are given in me
The vertical interval is 5

that the Iron Age tribe inhabiting this coast enjoyed a room with a view.

To the east is Bullslaughter Bay; is it named after a laughing bull or a slaughtered bull? There is a guillemot colony in the great gash on the tip of Mewsford Point. From here the official Coast Path runs too far inland to permit good views of the coast, but if you choose to walk along the cliff edge take great care.

As you approach The Castle you may notice a number of caves that are well above the limit of storm waves. Most have now been explored and in one or two there are traces of Stone Age human settlement. Between The Castle and Saddle Head the cliff scenery is superb and includes the deep gash

known as the Huntsman's Leap **75** – commemorating a famous huntsman who leapt over it on his horse but who then died of fright when he went back to check the width of the chasm

Soon you come upon St Govan's Chapel **76**, a diminutive building with an arched stone-vaulted roof, probably built in the 13th century. It has been carefully restored by the National Park Authority. From the chapel, if you wish to reach Bosherton, follow the road northwards for about 1¼ miles (2 km). Bosherton has a few cottages, a pub and a café, and is served by the Coastal Cruiser bus. The church is a typical Norman structure with a castellated tower, probably dating from the mid-13th century.

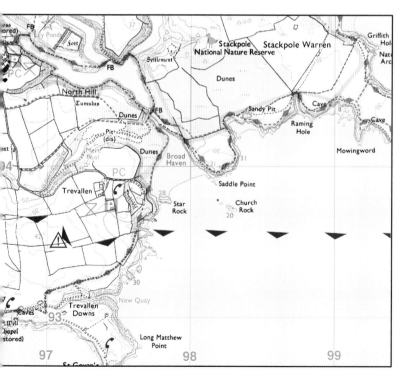

Grey seal pups are born on many Pembrokeshire beaches in the late summer and early autumn.

Coastal wildlife

The range of habitats along this coast is impressive because of variations in aspect and exposure; cliff profiles, which vary from vertical walls of rock to gently shelving sandy shores; and variations in rock type, which determine soil thickness, acidity and texture. Drainage conditions also vary from place to place; some cliff tops are reached by salt spray while others are not; and the influence of humans and farm animals is locally of great importance. As you walk the National Trail, you will encounter vertical cliffs, long cliff slopes masked with broken rock debris, storm-beach ridges, coastal mudflats, sand dune systems, salt marshes, freshwater lagoons, dense deciduous woodlands, as well as close-cropped grasslands and coastal heaths (in spring ablaze with flowers).

There is a succession of habitats in many cliff locations around the coastline. On the cliff faces, exposed to the full force of wind and salt spray, lichens may thrive but other plants seek the protection of gulleys and rock crevices. On the cliff top, maritime grassland is at its best in the spring when myriads of hardy flowering plants are in bloom, including spring squill, sea campion, thrift, ox-eye daisy and kidney vetch. Among the earliest of flowering plants are scurvy-grass, violet, celandine, primrose and cowslip. There is always some gorse in bloom, even in the middle of winter. By Whitsun the early spring flowers are joined by bluebell, campion and foxglove, and in May and June you will see spring and summer flowers all in bloom at the same time, with rocky cliff tops transformed into gaudy rock gardens.

In some clifftop areas there is a variety of coastal heath in which heather, gorse, bracken, blackthorn and bramble figure prominently. As the season progresses, the bluebells are overwhelmed by the vigour of bracken growth. Attempts have been made in recent years to restrict this growth through the reintroduction of traditional clifftop grazing, encouraging the expansion of areas of short grassland for the benefit of the chough population. There are scrub bushes and trees (including juniper and oak) in parts of this heathland and on exposed cliff slopes. In a few places sheltered from the westerly winds there are remnants of once extensive coastal woodlands, with oak, ash, sycamore, aspen, wild service, beech and many other tree species. The woodlands of Borough Head and Dale are typical.

The food resources of the deep clear waters off the Pembrokeshire coast and the abundant safe nesting places on remote cliffs, stacks and offshore islands have encouraged the growth of a large seabird population. On the island of Grassholm there are about 20,000 nesting pairs of gannets, and these majestic birds can often be seen from the trail, fishing close inshore. Puffins and Manx shearwaters nest in vast numbers on Skomer and Skokholm, and there is a sizeable colony of storm petrels on Skokholm. But perhaps the most familiar birds to be seen from the mainland coast are razorbills, guillemots, kittiwakes, fulmars, and various species of gulls. In addition there are colonies and small nesting groups of

shags and cormorants, and other nesting species to be seen on the cliffs include choughs, jackdaws, peregrine falcons, buzzards, ravens, feral pigeons, house martins and short-eared owls.

The most important mainland sites for watching cliff-nesting seabirds are the eastern side of Dinas Island (which is of course not an island) around Needle Rock, near the other Needle Rock some 1¼ miles (2 km) east of Fishguard, around Stack Rocks and Flimston Castles on the southern limestone coast, and to the west and north of Stackpole Head.

Over the decades there have been a number of changes in seabird distribution around the Pembrokeshire coast, mostly relating to declining numbers as human pressures on the coastline increase. Also, there is the ever-present threat of marine ecological catastrophes, such as that of the *Sea Empress* wreck, which spilled 72,000 tons of crude oil into Pembrokeshire waters and killed 40,000 seabirds in February 1996. But there are success

Gannets from the Grassholm nesting colony can often be seen fishing close to the Pembrokeshire coastline.

stories. The size of the gannet colony on Grassholm has steadily increased; the fulmar has spread around the whole of the Pembrokeshire coastline; the local chough population is holding its own; the peregrine falcon population is increasing; and there may also be an increase in the number of nesting sites used by house martins.

We should not forget to mention the other birds that are well adapted to life around the coast. Among the small birds are meadow pipit, rock pipit, skylark, linnet, yellowhammer and stonechat; all are common in open coastal habitats. In the sheltered patches of woodland you will see (and hear) jay, pheasant, wood pigeon, magpie, tawny owl, and even great spotted woodpecker. Yet another group of birds deserves attention, with many waders and ducks using the tidal mudflats as winter feeding grounds. If you visit the estuaries or the mudflats of Angle Bay or the Pembroke River you may well see great numbers of shelduck, teal, wigeon, mallard, oystercatcher, curlew, redshank, turnstone, dunlin and lapwing. The mute swan is the largest of the resident birds, but the heron is also very common, and in some winters Brent geese and Canada geese graze the coastal grassland.

Wildlife around the coast is dominated by the birds, but there are plenty of other animals. If you are lucky you may see foxes, and you should look out for badger setts along the whole of the route; otters live close to the footpath in densely wooded valleys, but you are more likely to see rabbits, and hares are becoming more common again after a period of decline. You may see mink, polecat, hedgehog and grey squirrel. Bats are quite common, nesting in many coastal caves and crevices; look out for them at dusk. Adders are also common along the length of the trail, and care is needed if you stray off the footpath and through dry heath vegetation in hot summer weather. Finally, keep an eye open for the less obvious members of the animal kingdom – in particular lizards, newts, frogs, toads, butterflies, moths and dragonflies near at hand, and grey seals, dolphins and porpoises in the sea down below. If you are lucky you may even see a basking shark . . .

The Bosherston Lily Ponds are man-made, but their lime-rich habitats support an abundant wild life of specially adapted plants and animals.

Cave near Linney Head, where the cliffs are made of thin-bedded limestone layers.

Cliff scenery around Linney Head

The clifftop area around Linney Down is made of white reef dolomites, quite different from the bedded grey limestone encountered along the rest of this coast. Once upon a time this was the site of a coral reef or atoll in a tropical sea. Notice the fine blowhole at the end of a deep gash in the cliffs. Linney Head is not as beautiful as it might be, but the view is wonderful and the limestone cliff scenery most impressive. The Head lies within the Ministry of Defence forbidden zone, and is particularly dangerous because it is a target impact area. It may only be accessed lawfully on a guided walk or by special arrangement with the Commandant. The sand dunes to the north have been used for live mortar and grenade practice.

Pen y holt Bay reveals some spectacular folding structures in the limestones. As you walk across Bulliber Down, Mount Sion Down and Flimston Down, look at the surface of the cliff top. The coastal platform is a classic example of a raised wave-cut platform, in this case 130 to 165 feet (40 to 50 metres) above present sea level. Probably it was formed during a period of relatively stable sea level about 40 million years ago.

Bosherston to Tenby

20 ¼ miles (32.6 km)
via Freshwater East and Penally

Ascent 2,920 feet (890 metres)
Highest point 269 feet (82 metres)

From Bosherston (served by the Coastal Cruiser bus) you may choose from two routes. It may be possible (firing permitting) to go south to St Govan's Chapel **76** and continue east on the Path.

If the St Govan's Head section of the National Trail is closed by the Army, it is always possible to walk via the car park down to the Lily Ponds, then via the northern footpath and footbridges to Broad Haven – also designated as part of the National Trail. The ponds **77** are beautiful, especially when the waterlilies and early summer flowers are in bloom. Created in the 18th century by the Earl of Cawdor to enhance his Stackpole Estate, they attract many birds. There is a large Iron Age fort on the tip of the peninsula between the two western lakes; it is reminiscent of The Gribin at Solva.

If you are intent upon following the coast, head eastwards along the permissive bridleway (also a wheelchair-accessible route) from St Govan's Chapel. Soon you come to Trevallen Downs, much disturbed by the Army during the Second World War. If you follow the National Trail you cut off St Govan's Head **A**, but this is not advised – the cliff scenery is too good to miss. The headland itself **78** is

riddled with caves, especially on the western flank of the peninsula. The little creek of New Quay is delightful – a deep inlet of crystal-clear water in the mouth of a dry limestone valley with white sand on the sea bed.

As you approach Broad Haven **79**, the Ministry of Defence entrance gate marks the eastern limit of the firing range. If the red flag is flying as you approach from the east, the range is closed and you will have to detour via Bosherston.

Broad Haven **79** (also served by the Coastal Cruiser bus) is a most attractive beach, with golden sands and a backdrop of sand dunes. On the edges of the dune system look out for the bright blue viper's bugloss, the pink and white restharrow (which looks like a sweet pea), and the bushes of sea buckthorn – one of the few plants that local naturalists actually *hate* because it spreads so rapidly and squeezes out other plant species.

The dunes of Stackpole Warren, now well stabilised, are still fed by sand blown up from Broad Haven. This has always been a great area for rabbits, with natural and artificial warrens used by rabbit-catchers until the 1950s. On the coast south of the warren look out

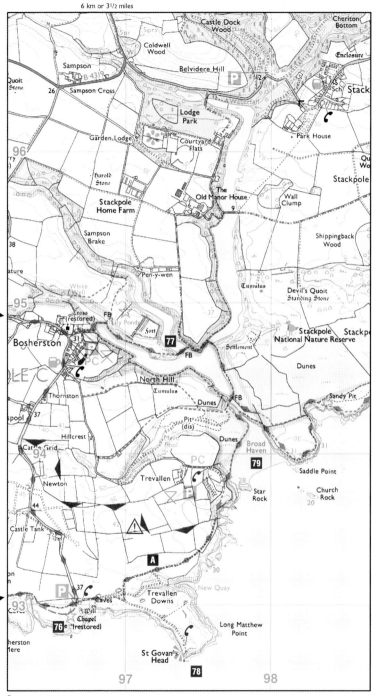

Castle Dock Wood

Cheriton Bottom

Coldwell Wood

Enclosure

Sampson

B 4319

Belvidere Hill

P

12

Sch

Stack

Quoit Stone

26

Sampson Cross

Waterfall

Park House

Qu
Wo

Lodge Park

96

Garden Lodge

Courtyard Flats

Stackpole

Harold Stone

The Old Manor House

Wall Clump

Stackpole Home Farm

9

Sampson Brake

Shippingback Wood

38

Pen-y-wen

ature

Tumulus

Devil's Quoit Standing Stone

White Well

95

Cross (restored)

FB

Lily Pond

Fort

77

Settlement

Stackpole National Nature Reserve

Stackp

Bosherton

31

P
PC

FB

Dunes

DLE C

North Hill

Tumulus

Sandy Pit

Thornston

Dunes

FB

37

pool

Pit (dis)

Broad Haven

94

Hillcrest

Dunes

Catt

Grid

PC

79

Saddle Point

Newton

Trevallen

Star Rock

Church Rock

44

20

Castle Tank

A

St Govan's Head

128

P

37

Caves

Trevallen Downs

New Quay

93

Wall Chapel (restored)

Long Matthew Point

76

herston
ere

St Govan's Head

78

97

98

Contours are given in metres
The vertical interval is 5m

A small lagoon at Broad Haven, near the outlet of the Bosherston Lily Ponds.

for nesting fulmars, razorbills, guillemots and choughs. If you wish to take a short route you can cut across the neck of Stackpole Head; however you will miss two huge arches punctured through the headland – the inner one is so high that quite large vessels can pass beneath it. The massive near-horizontal beds of pure limestone provide 'good-quality rock' for climbers, and a wave-cut platform exposed at low-water mark provides access to the base of the cliffs.

Barafundle **80** is totally unspoilt, remote and sheltered from the southwesterlies. There is no road access. Nevertheless, because it is consistently voted one of the most beautiful beaches in Britain, it can be very crowded during the summer. The wall on the north side of the bay was built by the Cawdors of Stackpole, and we can still imagine crinolined ladies flouncing their way down to picnics on the beach. In the area to the south of the valley, excavations by fieldworkers from the Dyfed Archaeological Trust and the University of Wales College of Cardiff have revealed prehistoric field walls, standing stones, Bronze Age settlement sites, barrows and other human burial sites.

Continuing northwards, you soon come to Stackpole Quay **81**, built by Lord Cawdor in the late 1700s inside an old limestone quarry. Limestone was exported by sailing vessels and coal was imported in great quantities for the heating of Stackpole Court, located some way inland above the eastern arm of the Lily Ponds. The National Trust took over 2,000 acres (806 hectares) of the Stackpole Estate in 1976, and careful management is a priority. The Trust has undertaken some interesting and sensitive building conversions near the quay, including a delightful café and tea room. Soon you come upon a very spectacular contact between the Old Red Sandstone rocks to the north and the Carboniferous Limestone to the south. Note how the cliffs change in colour.

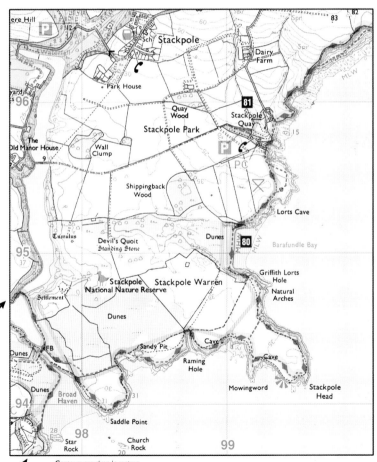

Contours are given in metres
The vertical interval is 5m

Passing Greenala Point you then reach Trewent Point, which affords fine views in all directions. You can either walk across the neck of the peninsula **B** or explore the outer part by a well-worn circular route that is popular with Freshwater East holidaymakers. Do not try to descend the northern slope by any of the smaller paths or you will end in the jungle! Pass Freshwater East **82** by going along the beach or through the dunes.

Then you continue eastwards along the cliffs, coming eventually to Swanlake Bay.

This is one of the most secluded and least-visited bays in Pembrokeshire, accessible by footpaths via West Moor and East Moor Farms. There is a seasonal tea room/café. Like Swanlake, Manorbier Bay has a fine wave-cut platform on its western flank, with a firm, sandy beach near the outlet of the stream. The castle dominates the northern side of the valley and the modern settlement is a little way inland. There is a pretty church with a tall Norman-style tower, and parts of the building are reputedly older than the castle. This was an

B4584 Lamphey
1 km or 1/2 mile

Contours are given in me
The vertical interval is 5

archetypal Norman manor, complete with priory, dovecote, fishpond, watermill, orchard and deer park. Gerald of Wales (Giraldus Cambrensis) was born here, probably in 1146, and it is from his writings that we know so much of his home settlement, which he called, naturally enough, 'the pleasantest spot in Wales'. Modern-day Manorbier offers a café, shop and inn, but parking is limited in the village. There is a large car park near the beach.

Barafundle Bay, one of Britain's favourite beaches, accessible only on foot or from the sea.

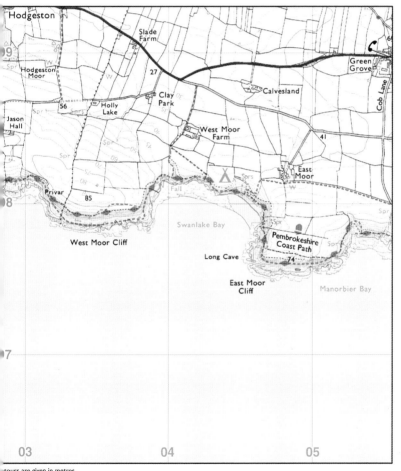

tours are given in metres
e vertical interval is 5m

Manorbier Castle, one of the best preserved of the medieval fortresses of Pembrokeshire.

Leaving the beach **C**, you come soon to the King's Quoit, a Neolithic burial chamber that demonstrates a nice piece of opportunism on the part of its builders. It is adjacent to an outcrop of coarse Old Red Sandstone exposed here in a near-vertical 'wall'. A large slab has fallen from this wall, and has been simply propped up with smaller slabs, providing a convenient burial place. Close to Priest's Nose there are several fearful chasms, up to 70 feet (20 metres) deep, probably caused by the picking out of bands of soft shale between beds of harder sandstone. Be careful when inspecting them. There is an even deeper chasm above the trail; it has sheer sides, and may be 100 feet (30 metres) deep.

Presipe is an attractive bay with golden sand, and rocks and stacks projecting through the beach. Access is via a steep flight of steps at the western end of the beach. However, Old Castle Head and its immediate hinterland are occupied by Manorbier Army Camp. In the 1980s the Army cleared many old buildings, reclaimed some land and released the area between the headland and the housing estate on the main road, permitting a realignment of the Coast Path **D**.

Follow the fingerposts around the fenced perimeter and when you reach the road, turn right and then left at the camp entrance gate. This road will take you to the old army building which has now been converted into a fine modern youth hostel with adjacent camping space. The National Trail actually runs closer to the coast.

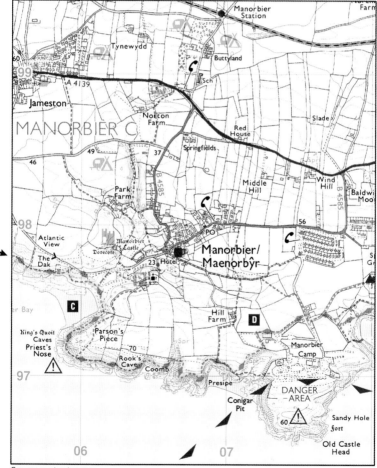

Contours are given in metres
The vertical interval is 5m

Skrinkle Haven beach **83** is not easy to reach! There are three beautiful coves here, separated by two large ramparts of limestone that project seawards from the main cliff line. Near the eastern set of steps there is a famous arch in the limestone cliffs called 'Church Doors'. If you descend by the steps remember you have to return, and they are steep! Also, it is all too easy to be cut off on the big beach as the tunnel from the small beach is flooded early when the tide comes in. Immediately above the bay, a sizeable area to the east of the youth hostel has been carefully landscaped so that old gun positions have become car parks, viewing points and picnic areas.

At the western end of the Lydstep peninsula, a limestone gorge coincides with a fault in the Carboniferous Limestone. There is a huge blowhole on the eastern flank of the valley, which

The limestone coast around Proud Giltar, seen from the beach at the south side of Lydstep Haven

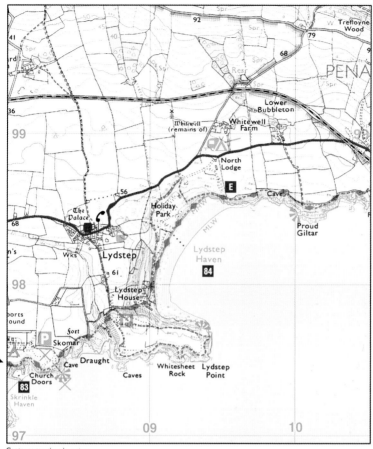

Contours are given in metres
The vertical interval is 5m

provides access to the Smugglers Cave. Other caves are accessible at low tide. The National Trust has laid out well-marked paths around the peninsula which provide excellent views of Giltar Cliffs and Caldey Island.

Lydstep Haven **84** has formed on the axis of a great east–west syncline or downfold in the Carboniferous Limestone. The beach is a splendid one, and was once incorporated into the elegant Lydstep Estate, with planted woodlands, copses and gardens. Now the place is transformed, with ranks of

caravans ranged up the slopes above the beach. Terraces, picnic areas, new roads, shops, car parks and holiday attractions are difficult to landscape, but the holiday company has made worthy efforts and Lydstep Haven could look a great deal worse. Follow the beach northwards and climb up on to the cliffs at the northern end of the bay **E**. Alternatively, follow the marked route through the caravan site.

Continue eastwards via Proud Giltar and Valleyfield Top. Access may be possible on to the small arms firing-range associated with Penally Camp. If so, continue eastwards towards Giltar Point – it is easy walking on springy turf. If the red flag is flying **F**, follow the National Trail towards Penally, passing under the railway and then turning right along the main road. Just past the station there is a right turn **G**. This path leads to South Beach, which you can follow into Tenby. If firing is taking place and this path is closed, continue along the main road then turn right towards the railway line. Walk beside the track until there is a right turn to Bacon's Hold, and from here go on to Tenby.

Penally is a pretty hillside village. The church contains an elaborately carved Celtic cross. Penally Abbey Hotel was once a religious house, and nearby are the ruins of the medieval St Deiniol's Chapel. The village has two village greens, shops, accommodation, pottery workshop and lots of flowers!

Assuming that you can follow the cliff top inside the firing range, continue to Giltar Point. As at Lydstep, limestone blocks could be loaded from the quarry here directly on to sailing vessels or barges that came and went with the tide.

South Beach **85** is a fine expanse of sand, backed by The Burrows. The dunes are oldest in the south and youngest in the north, where they have extended across the mouth of the Ritec Valley since

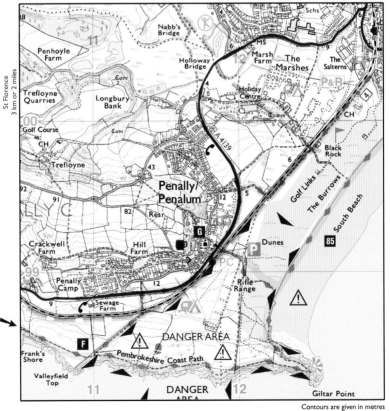

Contours are given in metres
The vertical interval is 5m

Contours are given in metres
The vertical interval is 5m

1811. Sea buckthorn is spreading like a plague over large parts of the northern dune area. The Ritec Valley was once an arm of the sea, providing medieval Tenby with superb natural defences. At that time ships are reputed to have been able to reach St Florence, 3 miles (5 km) inland.

Normally you can walk the length of South Beach on the sand, or along the junction between the beach and the dunes. Then, depending on the tide, you can either climb up the steps into the town, or follow the beach beneath South Cliff towards St Catherine's Island and Castle Hill. There are a number of access points up into the town. South Cliff provides a fine opportunity to examine a long run of limestone cliffs at sea level.

Priest's Nose, near Manorbier, where the Old Red Sandstone strata are standing almost vertically.

Tenby Harbour at low tide, overlooked by colourful Georgian town houses. Castle Hill is on the skyline.

Both Tenby and Saundersfoot are well served by daily bus and rail services. However, if you wish to use Saundersfoot railway station, remember that it is located some way inland of the village and the National Trail. Before you leave Tenby, I suggest that you have a look at the town and then resume your long-distance walk by following the good footpaths and roads that trace the cliff line around the built-up area.

The old town of Tenby **86** is tightly constrained within its medieval walls. Parts of the walls are in good repair, although their presence does create traffic problems. The massive South Gate

St Catherine's Fort at Tenby, overlooking part of South Sands

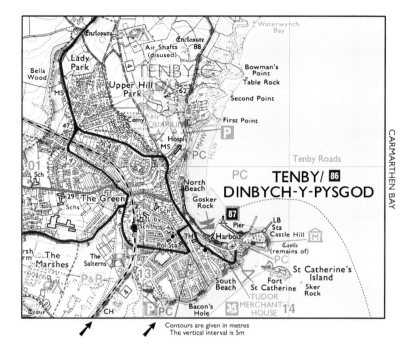

Contours are given in metres
The vertical interval is 5m

has been knocked about a bit over the years in order to allow traffic to pass through it; the resultant Five Arches form the town's most famous bottleneck. The ruins of the castle can be seen on Castle Hill, which also supports the town's excellent little museum. Other ancient buildings in the town include St Mary's Church, the largest medieval parish church in Wales; the Tudor Merchant's House; and the little fisherman's chapel close to the harbour. In Tudor and Stuart times Tenby was an important fishing and trading centre, and there were many powerful merchants in the town. Later the town became a popular health resort.

You can resume your walk on Castle Beach, between St Catherine's Island and the mainland. The island supports a Victorian fort, built in 1868–75 to provide an 'early warning' defence for the Milford Haven waterway. Just above

Castle Beach you can see the earliest lifeboat station, not surprisingly abandoned because of launching difficulties! Follow the footpath around Castle Hill, making a detour to visit the museum and the castle remains. On the north side of the hill, between the gas lamp standards, are the steps that led to the old Victorian Pier built in 1897. A little further along is the new (third) lifeboat station, not far from the second one.

The harbour **87** is a hive of activity when the tide is in. Follow the Promenade northwards along North Beach, and ascend to the cliff top via one of the flights of steps. Then follow the Croft northwards and continue along the road. The route now takes you inland. There are acorn waymarks on lampposts, leading you north until you reach the Coast Path proper.

Tenby to Amroth

Monkstone Point, which can be rounded on the beach if tidal conditions permit.

on the beach all the way to Saundersfoot. This route can only be recommended to those who are familiar with the tides in the area. If the tide still permits, you can continue all the way to Amroth (and the end of the National Trail) on the sand.

The Coast Path between Monkstone Point and Saundersfoot provides a pleasant walk, mostly through clifftop woodlands. Sometimes it is precariously close to the cliff edge, which is hidden by vegetation in places, so be careful. Because the south-westerlies are blowing across land there is no damage to the trees here from salt spray, and these ancient coastal woodlands are the most sheltered to be seen from the trail.

There is access to Saundersfoot beach beside the stream **D**. If the tide is high, take The Glen road, join the B4316 and follow it through to Saundersfoot. If you descend to the beach, detour a little way to the south to see the famous Lady Cave Anticline (a tight fold in the Coal Measures) before walking north towards the harbour.

Saundersfoot Harbour **88** was built largely for the coal-exporting trade. The village was insignificant until the 1800s, with most of the locally mined coal being exported from the beach. But then the growing demand for Pembrokeshire anthracite led to calls for a proper harbour, and building was commenced in 1829. Many of the local collieries were connected to the harbour by narrow-gauge railway tracks that ran through the village. One of these followed the coast via The Strand and through three railway tunnels en route to Wiseman's Bridge and Stepaside. This is the route followed by the National Trail.

At Waterwynch, a pleasant wooded valley dominated by a view of a large caravan park to the west, turn right if you want to visit the beach. Alternatively, follow the National Trail fingerposts through the larch woodland **A**; you will eventually regain contact with the coast. Continue through attractive sheltered clifftop scenery until you reach Lodge Valley, which is thickly wooded with larch and pine. The climb northwards out of the valley is very steep **B**.

At Monkstone Point there are a number of paths to choose from, but views are somewhat restricted by the coniferous woodland. One path leads out to the headland and provides the best views. A footpath with over a hundred steps descends to the firm sands of Monkstone Beach, but stick to the path and do *not* try to scramble down the unstable slopes **C**. Once down at beach level, you can scramble across the headland col and (tide permitting) walk

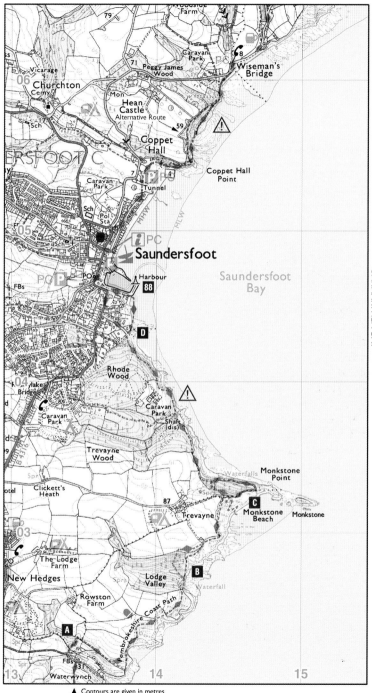

Contours are given in metres
The vertical interval is 5m

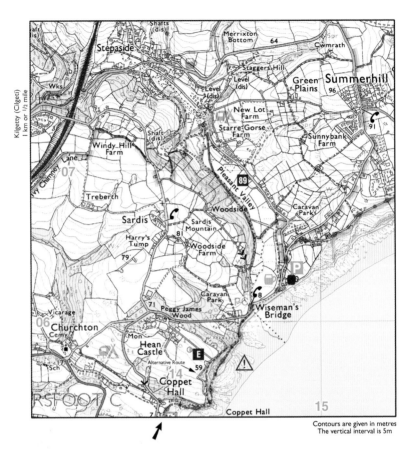

Contours are given in metres
The vertical interval is 5m

Storm beach and Coal Measures cliffs at Wiseman's Bridge, near Saundersfoot.

The Path to the north of Coppet Hall Point follows the route of the old railway track. The cliffs above it are notoriously unstable, with ironstones exposed in the Coal Measures. If this route is closed because of rock falls, it is possible to follow an alternative path along the cliff top **E**. At low tide, some walkers familiar with the tides choose to walk on the beach from Saundersfoot Harbour to Wiseman's Bridge. Pleasant Valley **89**, which runs inland towards Stepaside, was a centre of industry in the nineteenth century.

Follow the road past the Wiseman's Bridge Inn, climb the hill and bear right.

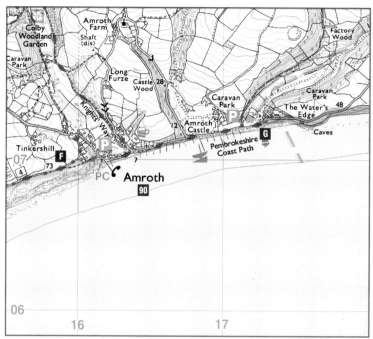

Contours are given in metres
The vertical interval is 5m

CARMARTHEN BAY

Eventually the road comes to an end and the Trail follows a bridleway which is surfaced as part of the Celtic Cycleway. The Path/cycleway now runs some way inland. As you approach Amroth you must turn right off the track **F** and cross the field, passing into a little patch of woodland and then descending into the village.

The final half-mile or so of your walk is on the road. Amroth **90** is a straggling village, which was originally a small miners' settlement. On the seaward side of the road are the storm-beach and coastal defences; the village wages constant war with the sea, and flooding is a danger when south-easterly gales coincide with high-water spring tides.

Amroth Castle is not a particularly ancient monument. There was a medieval castle here, but it has disappeared

without trace; it was replaced by the present building in the 18th century.

The National Trail ends at the mouth of the little stream **G** that also marks the boundary of the National Park. You have now walked, according to the rulebook, 186 miles (299 km). However, if you have followed my advice and explored all the headlands and various diversions along the way, you have walked at least 200 miles (320 km). Now you deserve a rest . . .

IIf you are determined to keep going, you can follow the Wales Coast Path (also the Carmarthen Bay Coast Path), which gives access to further fine cliff scenery at least as far as Pendine. Follow the road up the hill to the next footpath on the right and then head east. Also, take the relevant 1:25 000 map.

PART THREE
Useful Information

If you plan to walk on the Pembrokeshire Coast Path it is well worth looking at ⓘwww.pembrokeshirecoast.org.uk and at the dedicated National Trail site at ⓘwww.nt.pcnpa.org.uk. This site can also be accessed via ⓘwww.nationaltrail.co.uk which gives information on all National Trails in England and Wales.

Transport

For getting to Pembrokeshire by train:
ⓘ www.nationalrail.co.uk/planmyjourney
and by coach: ⓘ www.nationalexpress.com
For bus or rail services: www/traveline.org.uk or www.traveline-cymru.info
There is a very useful interactive map at: www.walkingpembrokeshire.co.uk.

Rail

There are good daily rail services between Pembrokeshire and the main South Wales stations, with intercity connections from Swansea and Cardiff to all parts of the UK. The main railway stations are at Haverfordwest, Milford Haven, Fishguard, Pembroke Dock and Tenby. Other stations are at Pembroke, Narberth, Kilgetty, Saundersfoot, Penally, Manorbier, Lamphey, Clunderwen, Clarbeston Road and Johnston. Stations to Milford Haven have the most frequent services. Stations to Pembroke Dock are served on a branch line via Whitland. Some trains to and from Fishguard and Pembroke Dock are timed to coincide with the comings and goings of the Rosslare services operated by Stena Line and Irish Ferries.

For timetable and other passenger enquiries, visit www.traveline.cymru.info or ☎ 0871 2002233. For regional train information please visit

ⓘ www.arrivatrainswales.co.uk or
ⓘ www.allpointswest.info

Buses

There is a daily National Express service between Haverfordwest and London, with coaches travelling via Milford Haven, Pembroke Dock and Tenby. There are also connecting services to most parts of the country from Swansea and Cardiff. Tickets for long-distance services should be bought in advance; book through Rapide offices or travel agents. Enquiries: ☎ 08717 818181.

The main towns are served by good daily bus services, and you are recommended to obtain a set of the County Council's excellent public transport booklets (which are free) in order to discover which points on the National Trail can be reached by bus. Most parts of the coast can now be reached by public transport, and matters continue to improve. Ring Traveline on ☎ 0871 200 2233. The walkers' shuttle bus services are particularly useful, providing access to a multitude of points on the National Trail. There are five services at present: Poppit Rocket, Strumble Shuttle, Celtic Coaster, Puffin Shuttle and Coastal Cruiser. There is a limited service in winter. Leaflets and timetables are widely available. Ring the Greenways Officer on ☎ 01437 764551
✎ greenways@ pembrokeshire.gov.uk
ⓘ www.pembrokeshiregreenways.co.uk

Places are sometimes available on morning and afternoon school bus services. Rural services now operate on a 'hail and ride' basis, which means that you can be picked up or set down anywhere on the route so long as it is safe to stop; in built-up areas designated bus stops should be used. For further information contact the County Council's Passenger Transport Unit on ☎ 0800 783 1584. If you want the timetable booklet for a part of Pembrokeshire (or a full set) write to the Transport Unit, Pembrokeshire CC Transport and Environment, County Hall, Haverfordwest SA61 1TP, or visit ⓘ www.pembrokeshire.gov.uk

Accommodation

Accommodation can be found in all of the main towns and villages on or near the National Trail, and in many farmhouses and isolated cottages along the route. Log on to ⓘ www.visitpembrokeshire.com for a free accommodation brochure. Most of the hotel accommodation is to be found in Tenby, Saundersfoot and St David's, but there are many smaller hotels and guesthouses which provide excellent and reasonably priced bed and breakfast facilities for walkers. Almost all accommodation providers now have their own web sites and accept internet enquiries and bookings. Remember that you are unlikely to find accommodation if you leave your booking until the last minute and if you want to visit Pembrokeshire at the height of the holiday season; advance booking and planning of your walk are essential. Even simple B & B accommodation in farms and cottages may be difficult to obtain 'on demand'.

The tourist information centres will help you to find accommodation, and all of the accredited centres operate a bed-booking service. There is also an ansafone service on ☎ 01437 763110, but for last-minute enquiries and bookings you are advised to search via the relevant websites.

For Tourist Information Centres see:
ⓘ www.visitpembrokeshire.com/TIC

Tourist information centres are at:

Cardigan: Tourist Information Centre, Theatr Mwldan, Bath House Road, Cardigan, Ceredigion SA43 1JY. ☎ 01239 613230.

Fishguard: Tourist Information Centre, Town Hall, The Square, Fishguard, Pembrokeshire SA65 9HE. ☎ 01437 776636.

Fishguard Harbour: Tourist Information Centre, Ocean Lab, Goodwick, Pembs SA64 0DE. ☎ 01348 874737.

Haverfordwest: Tourist Information Centre, Old Bridge, Haverfordwest, Pembs SA61 2EZ. ☎ 01437 763110.

Milford Haven: Tourist Information Centre, Suite 19, Cedar Court, Milford Haven, Pembs SA73 3LS. ☎ 01437 771818.

Newport: National Park Centre, Long Street, Newport. Pembs SA42 0TN. ☎ 01239 820912 (seasonal opening).

Pembroke: Tourist Information Centre, Commons Road, Pembroke, Pembs SA71 4EA. ☎ 01437 776499 (seasonal opening).

St David's: Oriel y Parc Gallery and Visitor Centre, St David's, Pembs SA62 6NW. ☎ 01437 725087.

Saundersfoot: Tourist Information Centre, Barbecue, Harbour Car Park, Saundersfoot, Pembs SA69 9HE. ☎ 01834 813672 (seasonal opening).

Tenby: National Park Information Centre, South Parade, Tenby, Pembs SA70 7LT. ☎ 01834 845040.

Tenby: Tourist Information Centre, Unit 2, Upper Park Road, Tenby, Pembs SA70 7LT. ☎ 01834 842404.

The main tourism offices are:

Pembrokeshire Coast National Park Authority, Llanion Park, Pembroke Dock, Pembrokeshire SA72 6DY. ☎ 0845 345 7275. ✎ info@pembrokeshirecoast.org.uk

Pembrokeshire County Council: Tourism Officer, PCC, County Hall, Haverfordwest, Pembs SA61 1TP. ☎ 01437 764551.

Visit Wales: Welsh Assembly Government, Brunel House, 2 Fitzalan Road, Cardiff CF24 0UY. ☎ 08708 300 306. ✎ info@visitwales.co.uk

The County Council publishes holiday guides and comprehensive accommodation lists that detail the locations, facilities and prices of all registered accommodation establishments in Pembrokeshire. Comprehensive Wales Tourist Board literature on caravan and camping sites and serviced accommodation is widely available. For a full list of this literature, contact the Visit Wales office (address above). Finally, various local guide books are widely available from shops, tourist information centres, guesthouses, cafés and petrol stations.

The following may be of use:
ⓘ www.welsh-cottages.co.uk
ⓘ www.coastalcottages.co.uk
ⓘ www.fbmholidays.co.uk
ⓘ www.qualitycottages.co.uk

Camping and touring caravan sites are identified on the Ordnance Survey maps in this book, but such sites come and go, and are carefully controlled by the authorities to ensure that minimum standards are met and to prevent uncontrolled growth in sensitive locations. Inevitably, a number of sites are not shown on the maps, and you are advised to obtain up-to-date lists from:

The Camping and Caravanning Club, Greenfield House, Westwood Way, Coventry CV4 8JH. ☎ 0845 130 7631.
ⓘ www.camping andcaravanningclub.co.uk.

The Ramblers in Wales: Ramblers Association Wales, Cymdeithas y Cerddwyr, 3 Cooper's Yard, Curran Road, Cardiff CF10 5NB; ☎ 029 206 44308.
ⓘ www.ramblers.org.uk/wales

Youth hostels

There are eight youth hostels in Pembrokeshire which can be used by members of the Youth Hostels Association. Further information and membership details can be obtained from the YHA, Trevelyan, Dimple Road, Matlock, Derbyshire DE4 3YH; ☎ 01629 592700. The youth hostels provide cheap and generally comfortable accommodation, but they are irregularly located around the Pembrokeshire coast and not all are on or near the National Trail. Also, remember that during the peak holiday period they are very crowded, and advance booking is essential if you are to be sure of a bed space.

For youth hostel information, visit the yha website at:

ⓘ www.yha.org.uk then contact the hostel of your choice.

The telephone numbers of the Pembrokeshire hostels are:

Poppit Sands, St Dogmaels (30 beds): ☎ 0845 371 9037.

Newport (28 beds): ☎ Newport 0845 371 9543.

Pwll Deri (32 beds): ☎ 0845 371 9536.

St David's, Llaethdy, near Whitesands, St David's (40 beds): ☎ 0845 371 9141.

Broad Haven (74 beds): ☎ 0845 371 9008.

Marloes (30 beds): ☎ 0845 371 9333.

Manorbier, Skrinkle Haven (68 beds): ☎ 0845 371 9031.

There are also a number of independent hostels, camping barns and bunkhouses: ⓘ www.independenthostelguide.co.uk.

Local organisations

In addition to the bodies listed above that deal specifically with tourism matters, there are a number of local organisations which contribute to the protection or management of the Pembrokeshire coast. They all have a role to play, not least in informing and educating the public on matters relating to the coastal environment. They need members and they need financial resources to enable them to act effectively in the protection of vulnerable sites and the encouragement of responsible visitor use.

Dyfed Archaeological Trust, Shire Hall, 8 Carmarthen Street, Llandeilo SA19 6AF. ☎ 01558 823121.

Wildlife Trust South and West Wales, The Welsh Wildlife Centre, Cilgerran, Cardigan SA43 2TB. ☎ 01239 621212.

Friends of the Pembrokeshire National Park, PO Box 218, Haverfordwest, Pembs SA61 1WR. ☎ 01646 680392.

National Trust (Office for Wales), Trinity Sq., Llandudno LL30 2DE. ☎ 01492 860123.

Other useful addresses

The following organisations are concerned with the protection of the environment and are responsible for the provision of public information.

Cadw: Plas Carew, Unit 5/7 Cefn Coed, Parc Nantgarw, Cardiff CF15 7QQ. ☎ 01443 336000

Environment Agency Wales, South West Area Office, Maes Newydd, Llandarcy, Neath SA10 6JQ.
☎ 08708 506506.

Countryside Council for Wales, Maes y Ffynnon, Penrhosgarnedd, Bangor, Gwynedd LL57 2DW;
☎ 0845 1306 229

Friends of the Earth (Cymru), 33 Castle Arcade Balcony, Cardiff CF10 1BY.
☎ 02920 229577.

Greenpeace, Canonbury Villas, London N1 2PN.
☎ 020 7865 8100.

Marine Conservation Society, Unit 3, Wolf Business Park, Alton Road, Ross-on-Wye, Herefordshire HR9 5NB. ☎ 01989 566017.

Pembrokeshire County Council, County Hall, Haverfordwest SA61 1TP.
☎ 01437 764551
ⓘ www.pembrokeshire.gov.uk

Royal Society for the Protection of Birds (RSPB), The Lodge, Sandy, Bedfordshire SG19 2DL. ☎ 01767 680551.

Worldwide Fund for Nature (WWF-UK), Panda House, Weyside Park, Godalming, Surrey GU7 1XR. ☎ 01483 426444.

Nearby places of interest

This guide has restricted itself to places on or adjacent to the Pembrokeshire Coast Path. However, further inland (and off the coast!) there are scores of sites of natural, cultural or historical interest which are popular with Pembrokeshire holidaymakers. To get a real feel for the character of the area, buy one of the local guide books and obtain a free copy of the National Park's *Coast to Coast* newspaper. Some local guides contain details of inland car tours which take in sites of particular interest. Here is a list of just 18 inland and offshore sites to whet your appetite:

Caldey Island Pembrokeshire's most popular island destination for holidaymakers. Cistercian abbey, ancient buildings, lovely beaches. Regular boat trips from Tenby.

Carew A lovely, tranquil place, with castle, old tidal mill and Celtic cross in close proximity. Not far away is Carew Cheriton Church, the finest rural parish church in Pembrokeshire.

Castell Henllys Iron Age Fort. An old fortified settlement with reconstructed huts, shop, education centre, and events on Celtic themes.

Cilgerran Welsh Wildlife Centre located nearby. An established and popular holiday venue. Award-winning visitor centre, nature trail, café and shops.

Cilgwyn Candles Workshop and Gallery This is one of many cottage craft enterprises in Pembrokeshire. Located not far from Newport, with candle-making demonstrations, mini-museum and upstairs gallery.

Cwm Gwaun This long and very beautiful valley stretches all the way from Newport to Lower Town, Fishguard. A sub-glacial meltwater channel, it separates the Carn Ingli upland from the main part of the Preseli upland ridge.

Foeldrigarn The finest Iron Age hill fort in Pembrokeshire, located on a summit at the eastern end of the Preseli Hills. Easy access from Croesfihangel, near Crymych.

Haverfordwest The county town situated right in the centre of Pembrokeshire at the head of navigation of the Western Cleddau River. Castle, ruined priory, old quays and warehouses, fine churches, and Pembrokeshire's best shopping centre.

Lamphey Palace Located not far from Pembroke, this is one of the Bishop's Palaces of Pembrokeshire. Splendid medieval architecture. The buildings are now looked after by CADW, the Welsh equivalent of English Heritage.

Llysyfran Reservoir Pembrokeshire's largest water-supply reservoir, built to provide process water for the Milford Haven oil industry. Country park, picnic areas, nature trail, shop/café.

Pentre Ifan Cromlech The most spectacular Neolithic burial chamber in Pembrokeshire, in a lovely setting. The massive capstone (supported by vertical stone pillars) is about 13 feet (4 metres) long.

Picton Castle A thirteenth-century castle which is still the home of the Philipps family. Woodlands, walled garden, gallery, café and shop.

Rosebush A small settlement with a fascinating history, located on the slopes of the Preseli Hills. Slate quarries and traces of the railway era are prominent, together with relics of abortive Victorian holiday developments.

Scolton Visitor Centre An old manor house now transformed into an attractive museum complex. Fine wooded grounds and country park. Frequent events are held in the grounds during the summer.

Skomer Island Skomer is a national nature reserve managed by Wildlife Trust South and West Wales. The island is magnificent, with spectacular birdlife. Visits are most worthwhile during the spring and early summer. Frequent boat trips from Martin's Haven.

Treffgarne Gorge and crags Located in the centre of Pembrokeshire, this is one of the area's favourite beauty spots. River, road and railway squeeze through the narrowest point in the gorge. Up above, on the skyline, are the tors of Lion Rock and Maiden Castle.

Y Felin, St Dogmaels A working water mill producing stoneground flour and other products. Visitors can see the mill machinery at work.

Bibliography

The Pembrokeshire coast is well blessed with literature describing it. The list that follows is by no means comprehensive, and new titles appear every year. There are bookshops in all the main towns of Pembrokeshire, and some tourist information centres and other outlets have selections of local books on sale.

Bennett, T., *Welsh Shipwrecks*, Vol. 2 (Laidlaw-Burgess, 1982).

Connop-Price, M. R., *Pembrokeshire: the Forgotten Coalfield* (Landmark, 2004).

Downes, J., *Folds, Faults and Fossils – Exploring Geology in Pembrokeshire* (Gwalch, 2011).

Driver, T., *Pembrokeshire Historic Landscapes from the Air* (RCAHMW, 2007).

Fishlock, T., and Moore, J., *Pembrokeshire: Journeys and Stories* (Gomer, 2011).

Green, J., and Roberts, O., *Birding in Pembrokeshire* (Welsh Ornithological Society, 2005).

Howells, R., *Old Saundersfoot* (Gomer, 1977).

Hull, L., *Castles and Bishop's Palaces of Pembrokeshire* (Logaston, 2005).

Jermy, R. C., *The Railways of Porthgain and Abereiddi* (Oakwood Press, 1986).

John, B. S., *The Rocks: Geology of Pembrokeshire* (Pembs. Handbooks, 2009).

—— *Pembrokeshire: Past and Present* (Greencroft Books, 1995).

Lloyd, T., Orbach, J., and Scourfield, R., *Pembrokeshire* (*The Buildings of Wales*), (Yale 2004).

Matthews, J., *Skomer – Portrait of a Welsh Island* (Graffeg, 2007).

McKay, K., *A Vision of Greatness* (Chevron, 1989).

Miles, D. (ed.), *A History of Haverfordwest* (Gomer, 1999).

Parker, R., *The Railways of Pembrokeshire* (Noodle, 2008).

Price, M. R. C., *Industrial Saundersfoot* (Gomer, 1982).

Rees, N., *St David of Dewisland* (Gomer, 1992).

Richards, A. J., *The Slate Quarries of Pembrokeshire* (Gwalch, 2012).

Scott, V., *In Harm's Way* (Paterchurch, 2000).

Sutcliffe, A., *A Tourist's Guide to the Pembrokeshire Islands* (Anna Sutcliffe, 1989).

Turvey, R., *Pembrokeshire: The Concise History* (University of Wales Press, 2006).

Wilson, D., *Pembrokeshire* (Graffeg, 2009).

Ordnance Survey Maps covering the Pembrokeshire Coast Path

Explorer (1:25 000): OL35, OL36
Landranger (1:50 000): 145, 157, 158
Motoring maps: Reach the Pembrokeshire Coast Path using the Road 6 Travel Map

Glossary of Welsh place names

Welsh place names are usually descriptions, some of them quite poetic. But the emphasis is on description. Many places begin with the word *aber*, meaning the mouth of a river. Aberystwyth, the mouth of the Ystwyth River; Abertawe (the Welsh name for Swansea), the mouth of the Tawe River. Another class of place name begins with the word *llan*, a church or parish. Llanfair, the church of (St) Mary; Llanfihangel, the church of (St) Michael.

Plurals in Welsh are usually formed by adding the letters AU to the end of a word, e.g. *dol* (a meadow); *dolau* (meadows).

A small Welsh–English pocket dictionary would be a useful companion in any walker's rucksack. But for the impecunious here is a small glossary of common words and their meanings:

Bach, *fach*, small	*Cefn*, ridge	*Dwr*, water	*Maen*, stone	*Pont*, bridge
Bryn, hill	*Clawdd*, dyke	*Dyffryn*, valley	*Mawr*, *fawr*, big	*Ty*, house
Bwlch, pass	*Coed*, wood	*Llyn*, lake	*Melin*, mill	
Caer, *gaer*, fort	*Du*, black	*Llys*, hall or palace	*Nant*, stream	

The Official Guides to all of

Cotswold Way

100 miles of quintessentially
English landscape

ISBN 978 1 84513 785 4

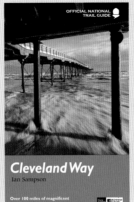

Cleveland Way

Ian Sampson

Over 100 miles of magnificent
walking on the North York Moors

ISBN 978 1 84513 781 6

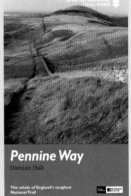

Pennine Way

Damian Hall

The whole of England's toughest
National Trail

ISBN 978 1 84513 718 2

Yorkshire Wolds Way

Roger Ratcliffe

A superbly tranquil walk through the
unspoilt chalk hills of East Yorkshire

ISBN 978 1 84513 643 7

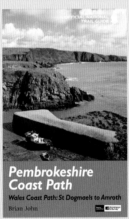

**Pembrokeshire
Coast Path**

Wales Coast Path: St Dogmaels to Amroth

Brian John

ISBN 978 1 84513 782 3

South Downs Way

Paul Millmore

100 miles of glorious chalk downland
for the walker, cyclist and horse rider

ISBN 978 1 84513 565 2

Hadrian's Wall Path

Anthony Burton

Follow the Roman Wall
from coast to coast

ISBN 978 1 84513 567 6

The Ridgeway

Anthony Burton

87 miles of downland walking
from Wiltshire to the Chilterns

ISBN 978 1 84513 638 3

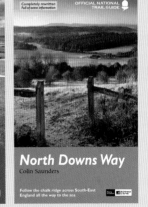

North Downs Way

Colin Saunders

Follow the chalk ridge across South-East
England all the way to the sea

ISBN 978 1 84513 677 2

Britain's National Trails

Thames Path
in the Country
David Sharp and Tony Gowers
From the source to Hampton Court

ISBN 978 1 84513 717 5

Thames Path
in London
Phoebe Clapham
From Hampton Court to Crayford Ness:
50 miles of historic riverside walk

ISBN 978 1 84513 706 9

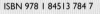

Peddars Way and
Norfolk Coast Path
Bruce Robinson with Mike Robinson
90 miles from Breckland to
salt marsh and sea cliffs

ISBN 978 1 84513 784 7

South West Coast Path
Minehead to Padstow
Roland Tarr
160 miles of coastal walking from
Exmoor to North Cornwall

ISBN 978 1 84513 640 6

South West Coast Path
Padstow to Falmouth
John Macadam
From golden beaches to rugged coves
around Britain's southernmost tip

ISBN 978 1 84513 641 3

Offa's Dyke Path
SOUTH: Chepstow to Knighton
Ernie and Kathy Kay and Mark Richards
Follow the ancient earthwork up the Wye
Valley and alongside the Black Mountains

ISBN 978 1 84513 561 4

South West Coast Path
Falmouth to Exmouth
Brian Le Messurier
171 miles of dramatic coves, cliffs and
beaches from Cornwall to Devon

ISBN 978 1 84513 564 5

South West Coast Path
Exmouth to Poole
Roland Tarr
From Jane Austen's Cobb to Lulworth Cove
– over 100 miles of historic coastline

ISBN 978 1 84513 642 0

NATIONAL TRAIL GUIDES
OFFA'S DYKE PATH NORTH
Knighton to Prestatyn
Ernie and Kathy Kay and Mark Richards

100 miles of walking through the
beautiful Welsh marches

ISBN 978 1 84513 312 2

PENNINE BRIDLEWAY
Derbyshire to the
South Pennines
Sue Viccars

ISBN 1 85410 957 X

Definitive guides to other popular long-distance walks published by

Aurum

WARWICKSHIRE
COUNTY LIBRARY

0136884441

A & H

796.51

£12.99

3605298

The Capital Ring
Colin Saunders

78 miles of green corridor
encircling inner London

ISBN 978 1 84513 786 1

West Highland Way
Anthony Burton

Ninety-three miles of Scottish moor
and mountain in Britain's most
spectacular long-distance walk

ISBN 978 1 84513 569 0

The London Loop
David Sharp with Colin Saunders

140 miles of secret countryside to walk
in a green corridor around London

ISBN 978 1 84513 787 8

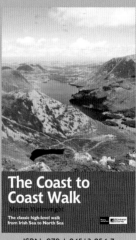

The Coast to Coast Walk
Martin Wainwright

The classic high-level walk
from Irish Sea to North Sea

ISBN 978 1 84513 854 7